3

19.00
.75E

FEB 1 4 1994

OCT   7 1994

APR 1 7 1995

NOV - 6 1995

NOV 2 9 1995

FEB 1 2 1996

MAR 1 5 1996
MAR 2 5 1997

NOV 1 0 1997

NOV 25/97

NOV 1 1 1998

NOV 6 2001
DEC 1 0 2001

MAR 2 0 2003

D1154086

ABOUT ISLAND PRESS

Island Press, a nonprofit organization, publishes, markets, and distributes the most advanced thinking on the conservation of our natural resources—books about soil, land, water, forests, wildlife, and hazardous and toxic wastes. These books are practical tools used by public officials, business and industry leaders, natural resource managers, and concerned citizens working to solve both local and global resource problems.

Founded in 1978, Island Press reorganized in 1984 to meet the increasing demand for substantive books on all resource-related issues. Island Press publishes and distributes under its own imprint and offers these services to other nonprofit organizations.

Support for Island Press is provided by Geraldine R. Dodge Foundation, The Energy Foundation, The Charles Engelhard Foundation, The Ford Foundation, Glen Eagles Foundation, The George Gund Foundation, William and Flora Hewlett Foundation, The John D. and Catherine T. MacArthur Foundation, The Andrew W. Mellon Foundation, The Joyce Mertz-Gilmore Foundation, The New-Land Foundation, The J. N. Pew, Jr. Charitable Trust, Alida Rockefeller, The Rockefeller Brothers Fund, The Rockefeller Foundation, The Tides Foundation, and individual donors.

Population, Technology, and Lifestyle

POPULATION, TECHNOLOGY, AND LIFESTYLE

The Transition to Sustainability

Edited by

Robert Goodland
Herman E. Daly
Salah El Serafy

ISLAND PRESS
Washington, D.C. ☐ Covelo, California

ERINDALE
COLLEGE
LIBRARY

© 1992 The International Bank for Reconstruction and Development and UNESCO.

All rights reserved. No part of this book may be reproduced in any form or by any means without permission in writing from the publisher: Island Press, Suite 300, 1718 Connecticut Avenue NW, Washington, D.C. 20009.

Library of Congress Cataloging-in-Publication Data

Population, technology, and lifestyle : the transition to sustainability / edited by
  Robert Goodland, Herman E. Daly, and Salah El Serafy.
    p. cm.
  Includes bibliographical references and index.
  ISBN 1–55963–199–6 (cloth : acid-free paper).
    1. Economic development—Environmental aspects.   2. Population—Economic
aspects.   I. Goodland, Robert J. A., 1939–.   II. Daly, Herman E.   III. El Serafy,
Salah, 1927–.
HD75.6.P67 1992
304.2—dc20   92–14403
                                                                          CIP

Printed on recycled, acid-free paper

Manufactured in the United States of America
10 9 8 7 6 5 4 3 2 1

Contents

Foreword

We were delighted to be invited to write the foreword for this book for four reasons. First, because it set a realistic and fair stage for the important United Nations Conference on Environment and Development (UNCED) 1992 meeting. Second, because it acknowledges that much more development is needed in the South. Third, because that needed development and growth must be accommodated by the North. Fourth, burden-sharing or reparation for the North's historic overuse of global environmental functions—both as source of natural resources and sink for wastes—is firmly accepted by the almost entirely Northern authors. This is refreshing.

We have not been too encouraged by the North's reaction to the Brundtland Report on sustainability during the five years since its publication. Therefore, we warmly endorse the clear thinking expressed in this book. The fact that two Nobel laureate economists—Trygve Haavelmo and Jan Tinbergen—are among the authors, raises our hopes that economists will push sustainability higher on their agendas for serious work in the 1990s. We fully share the authors' view that the transition to sustainability is urgent, and we find their suggestions on how to achieve it to be sensible. Now that UNCED 1992 is over, we must face the difficult part: mustering the necessary political will. That is up to each one of us.

EMIL SALIM
H.E. The Minister of State for
Environment and Population,
Jakarta, Indonesia

JOSÉ LUTZENBERGER
H.E. The Secretary of State for
Environment,
Brasília DF, Brazil

Introduction

At the outset, we want to acknowledge our major debt to the Brundt-land Commission's 1987 report, "Our Common Future." In particular, we greatly admire the Commission's achievement in garnering political consensus on the need for sustainable development. We use this report as our springboard, although we are far less comprehensive. Of the four elements of environmental sustainability—poverty, population, technology, and lifestyle—we focus on lifestyle, technology, and population, with that order of emphasis reflecting our skills. Poverty is only dealt with via our suggestions for a more equitable international income distribution. We acknowledge, however, that poverty and also debt are for some countries more pressing than environment.

Our aim is to follow Brundtland's lead concerning the need for a rapid transition to sustainability. We bolster Brundtland's case for the transition, because we feel that the need for this transition is not yet adequately recognized. We suggest specifics of what is needed to achieve the transition. We leave to others the more important task—namely, how to implement the transition; how to muster the political will for changes that will be painful but essential. We believe that understanding the necessity and general direction of the transition is a precondition for mustering the political will.

All authors have read and discussed each other's chapters and have reached consensus that the contributions included in this volume are not only compatible with each other but also mutually reinforcing. We collaborated for two reasons: first, because we felt that we all were already thinking along similar lines, judging from our previous writings, and second, because we all feel strongly that the next step for the transition to sustainability is agreement on the implications of what

Brundtland advocated. We have deliberately retained a certain overlap between some chapters in an effort to stress the notion that, regardless of the direction from which the subject is approached, the same conclusion is reached.

The conclusion is that economic activity cannot proceed any longer under the banner of "business as usual." Specifically, it is no longer tenable to make economic growth, as conventionally perceived and measured, the unquestioned objective of economic development policy. The old concept of growth, which we designate "throughput growth," with its reliance on an ever-increasing throughput of energy and other natural materials, cannot be sustained and must yield to an imaginative pursuit of economic ends that are less resource-intensive. The way we undervalue natural capital services and fail to account for natural asset degradation often means that we are impoverishing ourselves while imagining that our economies are growing. The new approach requires a concerted effort at remolding consumers' preferences and steering wants in the direction of environmentally benign activities, while simultaneously reducing throughput per unit of final product, including services.

Earlier studies of environmental limits to growth emphasized source limits (depletion of petroleum, copper, etc.). Experience has shown, however, that sink constraints (greenhouse effect, ozone depletion, local air and water pollution, etc.) are the more stringent. Since sink functions are common property to a greater extent than are source functions, this overuse is less correctible by the automatic market adjustment.

Acceleration of technological development is therefore required to reduce the natural resource content of given economic activities. We feel this important acceleration can be achieved in a way that will satisfy both the optimists as well as the pessimists. We suggest substantially increased taxes on throughput (such as carbon emission or mineral severance taxes). This should please the optimists because it will accelerate new technologies. It will please the pessimists because it will reduce environmentally stressful throughput. Since we must tax something in order to raise needed public revenue, why not tax the things we want to reduce (pollution and depletion) rather than the things we want to increase (employment and income)? Because pollution and depletion can never be reduced to zero, there is no danger of taxing our source of revenue out of existence, no matter how high the tax rate. As we gain revenue from these environmental taxes we can ease up on incomes taxes, especially on low incomes, even to the extent of using some of the new revenues to finance a negative income tax on very low incomes. We urgently call for fundamental changes in our economic objectives, as well as in our modes of behavior. Toward this end, the cooperation of all mankind is necessary.

Brundtland's call for sustainable development has elicited two opposing reactions. One is to revert to a definition of sustainable development as "growth as usual," although at a slower rate. The other reaction is to define sustainable development as "development without growth in throughput beyond environmental carrying capacity." World Commission on Environment and Development (WCED) leaders (Brundtland 1989, McNeill 1990) seem themselves to be torn between these two directions for operationalizing their concept.

Two realisms conflict. On the one hand, political realism rules out income redistribution and population stability as politically difficult, if not impossible; therefore the world economy has to expand "by a factor of five or ten" in order to alleviate poverty. On the other hand, ecological realism accepts that the global economy has already exceeded the sustainable limits of the global ecosystem and that a five-fold to tenfold expansion of anything remotely resembling the present economy would simply speed us from today's long-run unsustainability to imminent collapse. We believe that in conflicts between biophysical realities and political realities, the latter must eventually give ground. The planet will transit to sustainability: the choice is between society planning for an orderly transition, or letting physical limits and environmental damage dictate the timing and course of the transition.

While we agree with Brundtland that we should seek to limit, arrest, or even reduce the throughput associated with economic activity, we are far less sanguine about our ability to achieve this quickly. The vast expansion in economic activity projected by Brundtland is therefore bound to be associated with major rises in throughput. This does not involve any difference in theory between Brundtland and ourselves, but merely reflects the observable fact that successful substitution of man-made capital for natural resources is slow and limited, and that the necessary technology cannot be organized on cue as the optimists would wish.

Following the dictionary distinction between growth and development: *to grow* means to increase in size by the assimilation or accretion of materials; *to develop* means to expand or realize the potentialities of, to bring to a fuller, greater, or better state. When something grows it becomes quantitatively bigger; when it develops it becomes qualitatively better, or at least different. Quantitative growth and qualitative improvement follow different laws. Our planet develops over time without growing. Our economy, a subsystem of the finite and nongrowing earth, must eventually adapt to a similar pattern of development without throughput growth. The time for such adaptation is now.

An alternative formulation would be to say that physical input must cease growing, but that value of output can continue to increase as long as technological development permits. Of course, if physical input is limited, then by the law of conservation of matter-energy, so is physical output. This is equivalent to saying that quantitative growth in throughput is not permitted, but qualitative improvement in services rendered can develop with new technology. In other words, we are back to the formulation of development (increasing value of output) without growth (physical throughput constant). Throughput is treated as an aggregate, and clearly some components are more important than others environmentally. For many purposes, energy is the dominant and critical component.

Unfortunately, current gross national product (GNP) accounting conventions conflate growth and development, counting both as "economic growth." We sharply distinguish between throughput growth (growth proper) and efficiency improvement (development in the dictionary sense).

Once these distinctions are accepted it is reasonable to ask: Can development without throughput growth (sustainable development) cure existing poverty? Our belief is that it cannot. Qualitative improvement in the efficiency with which resources are used will greatly help, but will not be sufficient to alleviate poverty. The reduction of throughput intensity per dollar of GNP in some rich countries is all to the good, but means little to poor countries still striving for adequate food, clothing, and shelter. Basic necessities have a large and irreducible physical dimension, unlike, for example, information processing.

The Brundtland proposal to alleviate poverty by an annual 3 percent global rise in per capita income translates initially into annual per capita income increments (in U.S. dollars) of $633 for the United States, $3.60 for Ethiopia; $5.40 for Bangladesh; $7.50 for Nigeria; $10.80 for China and $10.50 for India. By the end of ten years, such growth will have raised Ethiopia's per capita income by $41—hardly sufficient to dent poverty there—while that of the United States will have risen by $7257. The greater disparity of international income levels that would result calls into question the desirability of Brundtland's projections.

It is neither ethical nor helpful to the environment to expect poor countries to reduce or arrest their development, which tends to be highly associated with throughput growth. Therefore the rich countries, which, after all, are responsible for most of today's environmental damage, and whose material well-being can sustain halting or even reversing throughput growth, must take the lead in this respect. Poverty reduction will require considerable growth, as well as development, in developing countries. But ecological constraints are real, and more growth for the poor must be balanced by negative throughput growth for the rich.

Development by the rich must be used to free resources (source and sink functions of the environment) for growth and development so urgently needed by the poor. Large-scale transfers to the poorer countries also will be required, especially as the impact of economic stability in rich countries may depress terms of trade and lower economic activity in developing countries. Higher prices for the exports of poorer countries therefore will be required.

Most importantly, population stability is essential to reduce the need for growth everywhere, but especially where population growth is highest—that is, in the poor countries.

Politically, it is very difficult to face up to the need for income redistribution and population stability. If the concept of sustainable development becomes a verbal formula for glossing over these harsh realities, then it will have been a big step backward. It is in this sense that we, the authors of this volume, are seeking to build on Brundtland before the tempest of conventional political "realisms" erodes the foundations that WCED constructed with such care and foresight. Such an agenda will be exceptionally difficult to implement, and many other issues are involved that are not addressed in this volume but of which we are acutely aware. Markets, for example, will have to learn to function without expansion, without wars, without waste, and without advertising that encourages waste. Economic policy will have to suppress certain activities in order to allow others to expand, so that the sum total remains within the biophysical budget constraint of nongrowing throughput. This adds up to a formidable political agenda. That is why exceptional political wisdom and leadership are so urgently required.

References

Brundtland, G. H. "Global Change and Our Common Future." Benjamin Franklin Lecture, Washington, D.C., 2 May 1989. *Environment (US)* 31: 16–20, 4–43.

McNeill, J. "On the Economics of Sustainable Development." Workshop, Washington, D.C., United States Agency for International Development, 23–26 January 1990.

World Commission on Environment and Development. "Our Common Future" (The Brundtland Report). Oxford: Oxford University Press, 1987.

Population, Technology, and Lifestyle

1

The Case That the World Has Reached Limits

Robert Goodland

Mahatma Gandhi [when asked if, after independence,
India would attain British standards of living]:
"It took Britain half the resources of the planet
to achieve its prosperity; how many planets
will a country like India require . . . ?"

The aim of this chapter is to present the case that limits to growth have already been reached, that further input growth will take the planet further away from sustainability, and that we are rapidly foreclosing options for the future, possibly by overshooting limits (Catton 1982). This chapter seeks to convince the reader of the urgent need to convert to a sustainable economy, rather than the related and equally or more important need of poverty alleviation. The political will to transit to sustainability will be mustered only when the need for the transition is perceived. The crucial next step—how to muster that political will—is deferred to a subsequent book.

To begin, plaudits for Brundtland's heroic achievement: elevating sustainability as a planetary goal now espoused by practically all nations, the United Nations family, and the World Bank. In July 1989, leaders of the Group of Seven major industrialized nations called for "the early adoption, worldwide, of policies based on sustainable development." The world owes Brundtland an enormous debt for this tremendous feat, and we admire her political wisdom. This chapter builds on Brundtland's lead and explores the implications of sustainability. We assume as given that the world is being run unsustainably now—being fueled by inherited fossil fuels is the best single example. Non-

3

renewable oil and gas provide 60 percent of global energy with barely fifty years of proven reserves.

Brundtland stated that meeting essential needs requires "a new era of economic growth" for nations in which the majority are poor. The report (WCED 1987) anticipates "a five- to tenfold increase in world industrial output." Two years later, this "sustainable growth" conclusion was reemphasized by the secretary general of the Brundtland Commission: "A fivefold to tenfold increase in economic activity would be required over the next 50 years" to achieve sustainability (MacNeill 1989).

The Global Ecosystem and the Economic Subsystem

A single measure—population times per capita resource consumption—encapsulates what is needed to achieve sustainability. This is the scale of the human economic subsystem with respect to that of the global ecosystem on which it depends and of which it is a part. The global ecosystem is the source of all material inputs feeding the economic subsystem and is the sink for all its wastes. Population times per capita resource consumption is the total flow—throughput—of resources from the ecosystem to the economic subsystem, then back to the ecosystem as waste, as dramatized in Figure 1. The upper diagram (A) illustrates the bygone era when the economic subsystem was small relative to the size of the global ecosystem. The lower diagram (B) depicts a situation much nearer to today, in which the economic subsystem is very large relative to the global ecosystem. Population times per capita resource use is refined by Tinbergen and Hueting (1992) and by Ehrlich and Ehrlich (1990).

The global ecosystem's source and sink functions have limited capacity to support the economic subsystem. The imperative, therefore, is to maintain the size of the global economy to within the capacity of the ecosystem to sustain it. Speth (1989) calculates that it took all of human history to grow to the $600 billion global economy of 1900. Today, the world economy grows by this amount every two years. Unchecked, today's $16 trillion global economy may be five times bigger only one generation or so hence.

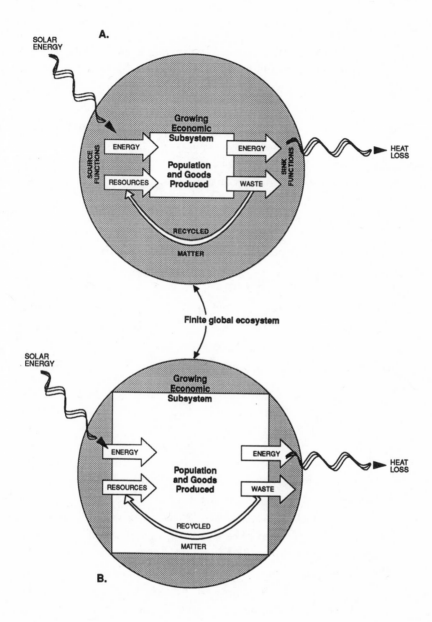

Figure 1. The finite global ecosystem relative to the growing economic subsystem (after Daly 1990a; Goodland and Daly 1990).

It seems unlikely that the world can sustain a doubling of the economy, let alone Brundtland's "five- to tenfold increase." We believe that throughput growth is not the way to reach sustainability; we cannot "grow" our way into sustainability. The global ecosystem, which is the source of all the resources needed for the economic subsystem, is finite and has limited regenerative and assimilative capacities. It looks inevitable that the next century will be occupied by double the number of people in the human economy consuming sources and burdening sinks with their wastes.

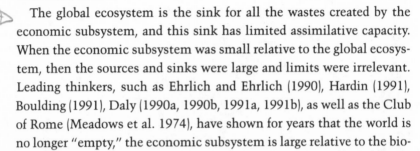 The global ecosystem is the sink for all the wastes created by the economic subsystem, and this sink has limited assimilative capacity. When the economic subsystem was small relative to the global ecosystem, then the sources and sinks were large and limits were irrelevant. Leading thinkers, such as Ehrlich and Ehrlich (1990), Hardin (1991), Boulding (1991), Daly (1990a, 1990b, 1991a, 1991b), as well as the Club of Rome (Meadows et al. 1974), have shown for years that the world is no longer "empty," the economic subsystem is large relative to the biosphere, and the capacities of the biosphere's sources and sinks are being stressed.

Localized Limits to Global Limits

This chapter presents the case that the economic subsystem has reached or exceeded important source and sink limits. We take as agreed that we have already fouled our nest: practically nowhere on this earth are signs of the human economy absent. From the center of Antarctica to the top of Mount Everest, human wastes are obvious and increasing. It is impossible to find a sample of ocean water with no sign of the 20 billion tons of human wastes added annually. PCBs and other persistent toxic chemicals, such as DDT and heavy metal compounds, have already accumulated throughout the marine ecosystem. One-fifth of the world's population breathes air more poisonous than WHO standards recommend, and an entire generation of Mexico City children may be intellectually stunted by lead poisoning (Brown et al. 1991).

Since the Club of Rome's 1972 report "Limits to Growth," the constraints have shifted from source limits to sink limits. Source limits are more open to substitution and are more localized. Since then, the case has substantially strengthened for limits to throughput growth. There is a wide variety of limits. Some are tractable and are being tackled, such as the CFC phase-out under the Montreal Convention. Other limits are less tractable, such as the massive human appropriation of biomass (see below). The key limit is the sink constraint of fossil energy use. Therefore, the rate of transition to renewables, including solar energy, parallels the rate of transition to sustainability. Here the optimists add the possibility of cheap fusion energy by the year 2050. We are agnostic on technology and want to encourage it by energy taxes (see Chapter 2). Hitherto, technology has only started to focus on input reduction and even less on sink management, which suggests there is scope for improvements.

Land-fill sites are becoming harder to find; garbage is shipped thousands of miles from industrial to developing countries in search of unfilled sinks. It has so far proved impossible for the U.S. Nuclear Regulatory Commission to find anywhere to rent a nuclear waste site for U.S. $100 million per year. Germany's Kraft-Werk Union signed an agreement with China in July 1987 to bury nuclear waste in Mongolia's Gobi Desert. These facts prove that land-fill sites and toxic dumps— aspects of sinks—are increasingly hard to find, that limits are near.

First Evidence of Limits: Human Biomass Appropriation

The best evidence that there are other imminent limits is the calculation by Vitousek et al. (1986) that the human economy uses—directly or indirectly—about 40 percent of the net primary product of terrestrial photosynthesis today. (This figure drops to 25 percent if the oceans and other aquatic ecosystems are included.) And desertification, urban encroachment onto agricultural land, blacktopping, soil erosion, and pollution are increasing—as is the population's search for food. This means that in only a single doubling of the world's population (say, thirty-five years) we will use 80 percent, and 100 percent shortly thereafter. As Daly (1991a, 1991b) points out, 100 percent appropriation is ecologically impossible and socially highly undesirable. The world will go from half-empty to full in one doubling period, irrespective of the sink being filled or the source being consumed. Readers refusing to recognize such overfullness that has appropriated 40 percent for humans already should decide when between now and 100 percent they would be willing to say "enough." What evidence will they require to be convinced? Although the Vitousek et al. evidence has not been refuted during the last five years, this single study is so stark that we urge prompt corroboration and analysis of the implications.

Second Evidence of Limits: Global Warming

Evidence of atmospheric carbon dioxide accumulation is pervasive, as geographically extensive as possible, and unimaginably expensive to cure if allowed to worsen. In addition, the evidence is unambiguously negative and strongly so. There may be a few exceptions, such as plants growing faster in CO_2-enriched laboratories where water and nutrients are not limiting. However, in the real world, it seems more likely that crop belts will not shift with changing climate, nor will they grow faster, because some other factor (for example, suitable soils or water) will become limiting. The prodigious North American breadbasket's climate may indeed shift north; but this does not mean that the breadbasket will follow, because the rich prairie soils will stay put, and Canadian boreal soils and muskeg are very infertile.

The second evidence that limits have been exceeded is global warming. The year 1990 was the warmest year in more than a century of record-keeping. Seven of the hottest years on record all occurred in the last 11 years. The 1980s were 1 degree Fahrenheit warmer than the 1880s, while 1990 was 1.25 degrees Fahrenheit warmer. This contrasts alarmingly with the pre-industrial constancy in which the earth's temperature did not vary more than 2 to 4 degrees Fahrenheit in the last 10,000 years. Humanity's entire social and cultural infrastructure over the last 7000 years has evolved entirely within a global climate that never deviated as much as 2 degrees Fahrenheit from today's climate (Arrhenius and Waltz 1990).

It is too soon to be absolutely certain that global "greenhouse" warming has begun: normal climatic variability is too great for absolute certainty. There is even greater uncertainty about the possible effects. But all the evidence suggests that global warming may well have started, that CO_2 accumulation started years ago, as postulated by Svante Arrhenius in 1896, and that it is worsening fast. Scientists now practically universally agree that such warming will occur, although differences remain on the rates. The U.S. National Academy of Science warned President Bush that global warming may well be the most pressing international issue of the next century. A dwindling minority of scientists remain agnostic. The dispute concerns policy responses much more than the predictions.

The scale of today's fossil-fuel-based human economy seems to be the dominant cause of greenhouse gas accumulation. The biggest contribution to greenhouse warming—carbon dioxide released from burning coal, oil, and natural gas—is accumulating fast in the atmosphere. Today's 5.3 billion people annually burn the equivalent of more than one ton of coal each.

Next in importance in contributing to greenhouse warming are all other pollutants released by the economy that exceed the biosphere's absorptive capacity: methane, CFCs, and nitrous oxide. Relative to carbon dioxide these three pollutants are orders of magnitude more damaging, although their amount is much less. Today's price to polluters for using atmospheric sink capacity for carbon dioxide disposal is zero, although the real opportunity cost may turn out to be astronomical.

The costs of rejecting the greenhouse hypothesis, if true, are vastly greater than the costs of accepting the hypothesis, if it proves to be false. By the time the evidence is irrefutable, it is sure to be too late to avert unacceptable costs, such as the influx of millions of refugees from low-lying coastal areas (55 percent of the world's population lives on coasts or estuaries), damage to ports and coastal cities, an increase in storm intensity, and, worst of all, damage to agriculture. Furthermore, abating global warming may save money, not cost it, according to Lovins (1990), when the benefit from lower fuel bills is factored in. The greenhouse threat is more than sufficient to justify action now, even if only in an insurance sense. The question to be resolved is how much insurance to buy?

Admittedly, great uncertainty prevails. But uncertainty cuts both ways. "Business as usual" or "wait and see" approaches are thus imprudent, if not foolhardy. Underestimation of greenhouse or ozone shield risks is just as likely as overestimation. Recent studies suggest that we are underestimating risks, rather than the converse. In May 1991, the U.S. EPA upped *by twentyfold* their estimate of UV-radiation cancer deaths, and the earth's ability to absorb methane was estimated *downward by 25 percent* in June 1991. In the face of uncertainty about global environmental health, prudence should be paramount.

The relevant component here is the tight relationship between carbon released and the scale of the economy. Global carbon emissions have increased annually since the Industrial Revolution, currently at nearly 4 percent per year. To the extent that energy use parallels economic activity, carbon emissions are an index of the scale of the economy. Fossil fuels account for 78 percent of U.S. energy. Of course, there is tremendous scope for reducing the energy intensity of industry and of the economy in general; that is why reductions in carbon emissions are possible without reducing standards of living. A significant degree of decoupling economic growth from energy throughput appears substantially achievable. Witness the 81 percent increase in Japan's output since 1973 using the same amount of energy. Similarly, the United States achieved nearly a 39 percent increase in GNP since 1973 with only a modest increase in energy use. This means energy efficiency increased almost 26 percent. Sweden—cold, gloomy, industrialized, and very energy-efficient—is the best example of how profitable it is to reduce CO_2. The Swedish State Power Board found that doubled electric efficiency, a 34 percent decrease in CO_2, and the phase-out of the nuclear power that supplies 50 percent of the country's electricity actually *lowers* consumers' electricity bills by U.S. $1 billion per year (Lovins 1990). Other, less efficient nations should be able to do even better.

Reducing energy intensity is possible in all industrial economies and in the larger developing economies, such as China, Brazil, and India. The scope of increasing energy use without increasing CO_2 means primarily the overdue transition to renewables: biomass, solar, and hydro. The other major source of carbon emissions—deforestation—also parallels the scale of the economy. More people needing more land push back the frontier. But there are vanishingly few geopolitical frontiers left today.

Greenhouse warming is a compelling argument that limits have been exceeded because it is globally pervasive, rather than disrupting the atmosphere in the region where the CO_2 was produced. In comparison, regional evidence of limits includes acid rain damaging parts of the United States and Canada, and those parts of Scandinavia downwind from the United Kingdom, and the "Waldesterben," or U.S. $30 billion loss of much of Europe's forest.

The nearly 7 billion tons of carbon released into the atmosphere each year by human activity (from fossil fuels and deforestation) accumulate in the atmosphere, which suggests that the ecosystem's sinks capable of absorbing carbon have been exceeded, and carbon accumulation appears for all practical purposes irreversible on any relevant time frame; hence it is of major concern for sustainability for future generations. Removal of carbon dioxide by liquefying it or chemically scrubbing it from stacks might double the cost of electricity. Optimistically, technology may reduce this cost, but still at a major penalty.

Third Evidence of Limits: Ozone Shield Rupture

The third evidence that global limits have been reached is the rupture of the ozone shield. It is difficult to imagine more compelling evidence that human activity has already damaged our life-support systems than the cosmic holes in the ozone shield. That CFCs would damage the ozone layer was predicted as far back as 1974 by Sherwood Rowland and Mario Molina. But when the damage was first detected—in 1985 in Antarctica—disbelief was so great that the data were rejected as coming from faulty sensors. Retesting and a search of hitherto undigested computer printouts confirmed that not only did the hole exist in 1985, but that it had appeared each spring since 1979. The world had failed to detect a vast hole that threatened human life and food production and that was more extensive than the United States and taller than Mount Everest (Shea 1989).

The single Antarctic ozone hole has now gone global. All subsequent tests have proved global ozone layer thinning far faster than models predicted. A second hole was subsequently discovered over the Arctic, and recently ozone shield thinning has been detected over both north and south temperate latitudes, including over northern Europe and North America. Furthermore, the temperate holes are edging from the less dangerous winter into the spring, thus posing more of a threat to sprouting crops and to humans. The incidence of blindness in Chilean sheep and Patagonian rabbits in the Andes soared in 1991.

The relationship between the increased ultraviolet "B" radiation leaking through the impaired ozone shield and skin cancers and cataracts is relatively well known—every 1 percent decrease in the ozone layer results in 5 percent more of certain skin cancers—and alarming in neighboring regions (for example, Queensland, Australia). The world seems destined for 1 billion additional skin cancers, many of them fatal, among people alive today. The possibly more serious human health effect is depression of our immune systems, increasing our vulnerability to an array of tumors, parasites, and infectious diseases. In addition, as the shield weakens, crop yields and marine fisheries will decline. But the gravest effect may be the uncertainty, such as upsetting normal balances in natural vegetation. Keystone species—those on which many others depend for survival—may decrease, leading to widespread disruption in environmental services and accelerating extinctions.

The 1 million or so tons of CFCs annually dumped into the biosphere take about 10 years to waft up to the ozone layer, where they destroy it with a half-life of 100 to 150 years. The tonnage of CFCs and other ozone-depleting gases released into the atmosphere is increasing damage to the ozone shield. Today's damage, although serious, only reflects the relatively low levels of CFCs released in the early 1980s. If CFC emissions cease today, the world still will be gripped in an unavoidable commitment to 10 years of increased damage. This would then gradually return to predamage levels over the next 100 to 150 years.

This seems to be evidence that the global ecosystem's sink capacity to absorb CFC pollution has been vastly exceeded. The limits have been reached and exceeded; mankind is in for damage to environmental services, human health, and food production. This is a good example because 85 percent of CFCs are released in the industrial North, but the main hole appeared over Antarctica in the ozone layer twenty kilometers up in the sky, showing the damage to be widespread and truly global in nature.

Fourth Evidence of Limits: Land Degradation

Land degradation—decreased productivity such as caused by accelerated soil erosion, salination, and desertification—is only one of the many topics that could be included here. It is not new; land degraded thousands of years ago (for example, the Tigris-Euphrates Valley) remains unproductive today. But the scale has mushroomed and is important because practically all (97 percent) food comes from land rather than from aquatic or ocean systems. As 35 percent of the earth's land already is degraded, and since this figure is increasing and is largely irreversible in any time scale of concern to society, such degradation is a sign that we have exceeded the regenerative capacity of the earth's soil source.

Pimentel et al. (1987) found that soil erosion is serious in most of the world's agricultural areas and that this problem is worsening as more marginal land is brought into production. Soil loss rates, generally ranging from 10 to 100 tons per hectare per year, exceed soil formation rates by at least tenfold. Agriculture is leading to erosion, salination, or waterlogging of possibly 6 million hectares per year: "a crisis seriously affecting the world food economy."

Exceeding the limits of this particular environmental source function raises food prices and exacerbates income inequality at a time when 1 billion people are already malnourished. As one-third of developing-country populations now face fuel wood deficits, crop residues and dung are diverted from agriculture to fuel. Fuel wood overharvesting and this diversion intensify land degradation, hunger, and poverty.

Fifth Evidence of Limits: Decrease in Biodiversity

The scale of the human economy has grown so large that there is no longer room for all species in the ark. The rates of takeover of wildlife habitat and of species extinctions are the fastest they have ever been in recorded history and are accelerating. The world's richest species habitat, tropical forest, has already been 55 percent destroyed; the current rate exceeds 168,000 square kilometers per year. As the total number of species extant is not yet known to the nearest order of magnitude (5 million or 30 million or more), it is impossible to determine precise extinction rates. However, conservative estimates put the rate at more than 5000 species of our inherited genetic library irreversibly extinguished each year. This is about 10,000 times as fast as prehuman extinction rates. Less conservative estimates put the rate at 150,000 species per year (Goodland 1991). Many find such anthropocentrism to be arrogant and immoral. It also increases risks of overshoot. Built-in redundancy is a part of many biological systems, but we do not know how near thresholds are. Most extinctions from tropical deforestation (for example, colonization) today increase poverty—tropical moist forest soils are fragile—so we do not even have much of a beneficial trade-off with development here.

Population

Brundtland is sensible on population: adequate food is too expensive for one-fourth of the earth's population today. Birthweight is declining in places. Poverty stimulates population growth. Direct poverty alleviation is essential; "business as usual" on poverty alleviation is immoral. MacNeill (1989) states it plainly: "reducing rates of population growth" is an essential condition to achieve sustainability. This is as important, if not more so, in industrial countries as it is in developing countries. Industrial countries overconsume per capita, hence overpollute, and thus are responsible for by far the largest share of limits being reached. The richest 20 percent of the world consumes more than 70 percent of the world's commercial energy. Thirteen nations already have achieved zero population growth, so it is not utopian to expect others to follow.

Developing countries contribute to exceeding limits because they are so populous today (77 percent of the world's total) and are increasing far faster than their economies can provide for them (90 percent of world population growth). Real incomes are declining in some areas. If left unchecked, it may be halfway through the twenty-first century before the number of births will fall back even to current high levels. Developing-countries' population growth alone would account for a 75 percent increase in their commercial energy consumption by 2025, even if per capita consumption remained at current inadequate levels (OTA 1991). These countries need so much growth due to the population increase that this can be freed up only by the transition to sustainability in industrial countries.

The poor must be given the chance, must be assisted, and will justifiably demand to reach at least minimally acceptable living standards by access to the remaining natural resource base. When industrial nations switch from input growth to qualitative development, more resources and environmental functions will be available for the South's needed growth. This is a major role of the World Bank. It is in the interests of developing countries and the world commons not to follow the fossil fuel model. It is in the interests of industrial countries to subsidize alternatives, and this is an increasing role for the World Bank. This view is repeated by Dr. Qu Wenhu, of Academica Sinica, who says: "If 'needs' includes one automobile for each of a billion Chinese, then sustainable development is impossible." Developing-countries' populations account for only 17 percent of total commercial energy now, but unchecked this will almost double by 2020 (OTA 1991).

Merely meeting the unmet demand for family planning would help enormously. Educating girls and providing them with credit for productive purposes and employment opportunities are probably the next most effective measures. A full 25 percent of U.S. births, and a much larger number of developing-country births, are to unmarried mothers, hence providing less child care. Most of these births are unwanted, which also tends to result in less care. Certainly, international development agencies should assist high-population-growth countries in reducing to world averages as an urgent first step, instead of trying only to increase infrastructure without population measures.

Growth Versus Development

To the extent that the economic subsystem has indeed become large relative to the global ecosystem on which it depends, and the regenerative and assimilative capacities of its sources and sinks are being exceeded, then the growth called for by Brundtland will dangerously exacerbate surpassing the limits outlined above. Opinions differ. MacNeill (1989) claims "a minimum of 3% annual per capita income growth is needed to reach sustainability during the first part of the next century," and this would need higher growth in national income, given population trends. Hueting (1990) disagrees, concluding that for sustainability "what we need **least** is an increase in national income." Sustainability will be achieved only to the extent that quantitative throughput growth stabilizes and is replaced by qualitative development, holding inputs constant. Reverting to the scale of the economy—population times per capita resource use—per capita resource use must decline, as well as population.

Brundtland is excellent on three of the four necessary conditions for sustainability. First, the production of more with less (for example, conservation, efficiency, technological improvements, and recycling). Japan excels in this regard, producing 81 percent more real output than it did in 1973 using the same amount of energy. Second, the reduction of the population explosion. Third, the redistribution from overconsumers to the poor. Brundtland was probably being politically astute in leaving fuzzy the fourth necessary condition to make all four sufficient to reach sustainability. This is the transition from input growth and growth in the scale of the economy to qualitative development, holding the scale of the economy consistent with the regenerative and assimilative capacities of global life-support systems. In several places the Brundtland Report hints at this. In qualitative, sustainable development, production replaces depreciated assets, and births replace deaths, so that stocks of wealth and people are continually renewed and even improved (Daly 1990b). A developing economy is getting better: the well-being of the (stable) population improves. An economy growing in throughput is getting bigger, exceeding limits, and damaging the self-repairing capacity of the planet.

To the extent our leaders recognize the fact that the earth has reached limits and decide to reduce further expansion in the scale of the economy, we must prevent hardship in this tremendous transition for poor countries. Brundtland commendably advocates growth for poor countries. But only raising the bottom without lowering the top will not permit sustainability (Haavelmo 1990).

The poor need an irreducible minimum of basics: food, clothing, and shelter. These basics require throughput growth for poor countries, with compensating reductions in such growth in rich countries. Apart from colonial resource drawdowns, industrial country growth historically has increased markets for developing countries' raw materials, hence presumably benefiting poor countries, but it is industrial country growth that has to contract to free up ecological room for the minimum growth needed in poor country economies. Tinbergen and Hueting (1992) put it plainest: "no further production growth in rich countries." All approaches to sustainability must internalize this constraint if the crucial goals of poverty alleviation and halting damage to global life-support systems are to be approached.

Conclusion

When economies change from agrarian through industrial to more service-oriented, then smokestack throughput growth may improve to growth less damaging of sources and sinks: from coal and steel to fiber optics and electronics, for example. We must speed to production that is less throughput-intensive. We must accelerate technical improvements in resource productivity—Brundtland's "producing more with less." Presumably this is what the Brundtland Commission and subsequent follow-up authors (for example, MacNeill 1989) label "growth, but of a different kind." Vigorous promotion of this trend will indeed help the transition to sustainability and is probably essential. It is also largely true that conservation and efficiency improvements and recycling are profitable and will become much more so the instant environmental externalities (for example, carbon dioxide emissions) are internalized.

But this approach will be insufficient for four reasons. First, all growth consumes resources and produces wastes, even Brundtland's unspecified new type of growth. To the extent that we have reached limits to the ecosystem's regenerative and assimilative capacities, throughput growth exceeding such limits will not herald sustainability. Second, the size of the service sector relative to the production of goods has limits. Third, even many services are fairly throughput-intensive, including tourism, universities, and hospitals. Fourth, and highly significant, less throughput-intensive growth is "hi-tech"; hence the places where there has to be more growth—tiny, impoverished, developing-country economies—are less likely to be able to afford Brundtland's "new" growth.

Part of the answer will be massive technology transfer from industrial countries to developing countries to offer them whatever throughput-neutral or throughput-minimal technologies are available. This transfer is presaged by the U.S. $1.5 billion Global Environment Facility of the United Nations Environment Program (UNEP), the United Nations Development Program (UNDP), and the World Bank that will start in 1991 to finance improvements not yet fully "economic," but which benefit the global commons.

This chapter is not primarily about how to approach sustainability: that is well documented elsewhere (Adams 1990, Agarwal and Narain 1990, Chambers et al. 1990, Conroy and Litvinoff 1988, Goldsmith, Hildyard, and Bunyard 1990). Nor is it about the economic and political difficulties of reaching sustainability, such as the pricing of the infinite (the ozone shield, for example), the endlessly debatable (biodiversity, for example), or pricing for posterity what we cannot price today. That is admirably argued by Daly and Cobb (1989), Daly (1990a, 1991a, 1991b), El Serafy (1991), and Costanza (1991). It is about the need to recognize the imminence of limits to throughput growth, while alleviating poverty in the world. Many local thresholds have been broached because of population pressures and poverty; global thresholds are being broached by industrial countries' overconsumption.

To conclude on an optimistic note: the Organization for Economic Cooperation and Development (OECD) found in 1984 that environmental expenditures are good for the economy and good for employment. The 1988 Worldwatch study (Brown 1988) speculated that most sustainability could be achieved by the year 2000 with additional annual expenditures increasing gradually to U.S. $150 billion in 2000. Money is available: World Bank President Barber Conable calculated early in 1991 that industrial country trade barriers cost developing countries about U.S. $100 billion in foregone income—twice the interest paid annually by developing countries on their international debt. Most measures needed to approach sustainability are beneficial also for other reasons (fuel efficiency, for example). The world's nations have annually funded UNEP with about U.S. $30 million, although they propose now "to consider" increasing this sum to U.S. $100 million. It is not financial capital shortage that limits the economy anymore. It is shortages of both natural capital as well as of political will in the industrialized world. Yet we fail to follow economic logic and invest in the limiting factor.

Many nations spend less on environment, health, education, and welfare than they do on arms, which now annually total U.S. $1 trillion worldwide. Global security is increasingly prejudiced by source and sink constraints as recent natural resource wars have shown, such as the 1974 "cod" war between the United Kingdom and Iceland, the 1969 "football" war between overpopulated El Salvador and underpopulated Honduras, and the 1991 Persian Gulf war. As soon as damage to global life-support systems is perceived as far riskier than military threats, more prudent reallocation will promptly follow.

Acknowledgments

I acknowledge the useful comments of Paul Ehrlich, Stein Hansen, Roefie Hueting, Frederik van Bolhuis, Sandra Postel, Jane Pratt, and Richard Norgaard.

References

Adams, W. M. *Green Development: Environment and Sustainability in the Third World.* London: Routledge, 1990.

Agarwal, A., and S. Narain. *Towards Green Villages.* Delhi: Center for Science and Environment, 1990.

Arrhenius, E., and T. W. Waltz. *The Greenhouse Effect: Implications for Economic Development.* Discussion Paper 78. Washington, D.C.: World Bank, 1990.

Boulding, K. "Ecological Paramountcy." In *Ecological Economics,* edited by R. Costanza. New York: Columbia University Press, 1991.

Brown, L. R., et al. *State of the World.* Washington, D.C.: Worldwatch Institute, 1988. (See also *State of the World* for 1989, 1990, and 1991.)

Catton, W. R. *Overshoot: The Ecological Basis of Revolutionary Change.* Chicago: University of Illinois Press, 1982.

Chambers, R., N. C. Saxena, and T. Shah. *To the Hands of the Poor.* London: Intermediate Technology, 1990.

Conroy, C., and M. Litvinoff. *The Greening of Aid: Sustainable Livelihoods in Practice.* London: Earthscan, 1988.

Costanza, R., ed. *Ecological Economics: The Science and Management of Sustainability.* New York: Columbia University Press, 1991.

Court, T. de la. *Beyond Brundtland: Green Development in the 1990s.* London: Zed Books, 1990.

Daily, G. C., and P. R. Ehrlich. "An Exploratory Model of the Impact of Rapid Climate Change on the World Food Situation." *Proceedings Royal Society* (1990): 232–44.

Daly, H. E. "Toward Some Operational Principles of Sustainable Development." *Ecological Economics* 2(1990): 1–6.

Daly, H. E. "Boundless Bull." *Gannett Center Journal* 4(3)(1990): 113–18.

Daly, H. E. "Ecological Economics and Sustainable Development." In *Ecological Physical Chemistry,* edited by C. Rossi and E. Tiezzi. Amsterdam: Elsevier, 1991.

Daly, H. E. "Towards an Environmental Macroeconomics." In *Ecological Economics,* edited by R. Costanza. New York: Columbia University Press, 1991.

Daly, H. E. "Sustainable Development: From Conceptual Theory Towards Operational Principles." *Population and Development Review.* Forthcoming.

Daly, H. E., and J. B. Cobb. *For the Common Good: Redirecting the Economy Toward Community, the Environment, and a Sustainable Future.* Boston: Beacon Press, 1989.

Ehrlich, P. "The Limits to Substitution: Meta-Resource Depletion and a New Economic-Ecologic Paradigm." *Ecological Economics* 1(1)(1989): 9–16.

Ehrlich, P., and A. Ehrlich. *The Population Explosion.* New York: Simon and Schuster, 1990.

El Serafy, S. "The Environment as Capital." In *Ecological Economics,* edited by R. Costanza. New York: Columbia University Press, 1991.

Foy, G. "Economic Sustainability and the Preservation of Environmental Assets." *Environmental Management* 14(6)(1990): 771–78.

Goldsmith, E., N. Hildyard, and P. Bunyard. *5000 Days to Save the Planet.* London: Hamlyn, 1990.

Goodland, R. *Tropical Deforestation: Solutions, Ethics and Religion.* Environment Department Working Paper 43. Washington, D.C.: World Bank, 1991.

Goodland, R., E. Asibey, J. Post, and M. Dyson. "Tropical Moist Forest Management: The Urgency of Transition to Sustainability." *Environmental Conservation* 17(4)(1991): 303–18.

Goodland, R., and G. Ledec. "Neoclassical Economics and Sustainable Development." *Ecological Modelling* 38(1987): 19–46.

Goodland, R., and H. E. Daly. "The Missing Tools [for Sustainability]." In *Planet Under Stress: The Challenge of Global Change,* edited by C. Mungall and D. J. McLaren. Toronto: Oxford University Press, 1990.

Haavelmo, T. "The Big Dilemma, International Trade and the North-South Cooperation." In *Economic Policies for Sustainable Development.* Manila: Asian Development Bank, 1990.

Hardin, G. "Paramount Positions in Ecological Economics." In *Ecological Economics,* edited by R. Costanza. New York: Columbia University Press, 1991.

Hueting, R. "The Brundtland Report: A Matter of Conflicting Goals." *Ecological Economics* 2(2)(1990): 109–18.

Lovins, A. B. "Does Abating Global Warming Cost or Save Money?" *Rocky Mountain Institute* 6(3)(1990): 1–3.

MacNeill, J. "Strategies for Sustainable Development." *Scientific American* 261(3)(1989): 154–65.

Meadows, D. H., et al. *The Limits to Growth: A Report for the Club of Rome's Project on the Predicament of Mankind.* 2d ed. New York: Universe Books, 1974.

Office of Technology Assessment. *Energy in Developing Countries.* Washington, D.C.: OTA, 1991.

Pimentel, D., et al. "World Agriculture and Soil Erosion." *BioScience* 37(4)(1987): 277–83.

Shea, C. P. "Protecting Life on Earth: Steps to Save the Ozone Layer." Worldwatch Paper No. 87. Washington, D.C.: Worldwatch Institute, 1989.

Speth, J. G. "A Luddite Recants: Technological Innovation and the Environment." *The Amicus Journal* (Spring 1989): 3–5.

Tinbergen, J., and R. Hueting. "GNP and Market Prices: Wrong Signals for Sustainable Economic Success That Mask Environmental Destruction." (Chapter 4 of this volume.)

Vitousek, Peter M., et al. "Human Appropriation of the Products of Photosynthesis." *BioScience* 34(6)(1986): 368–73.

World Commission on Environment and Development. "Our Common Future" (The Brundtland Report). Oxford: Oxford University Press, 1987.

2

From Empty-world Economics to Full-world Economics: Recognizing an Historical Turning Point in Economic Development

Herman E. Daly

The evolution of the human economy has passed from an era in which manmade capital was the limiting factor in economic development to an era in which remaining natural capital has become the limiting factor. Economic logic tells us that we should maximize the productivity of the scarcest (limiting) factor, as well as try to increase its supply. This means that economic policy should be designed to increase the productivity of natural capital and its total amount, rather than to increase the productivity of manmade capital and its accumulation, as was appropriate in the past when it was the limiting factor. This chapter aims to give some reasons for believing this "new era" thesis and to consider some of the far-reaching policy changes that it would entail, both for development in general and for the multilateral development banks in particular.

Why the Turning Point Has Not Been Noticed

Why has this transformation from a world relatively empty of human beings and manmade capital to a world relatively full of these not been noticed by economists? If such a fundamental change in the pattern of scarcity is real, as I think it is, then how could it be overlooked by economists, whose job is to pay attention to the pattern of scarcity? Some economists—for example, Boulding[1] and Georgescu-Roegen[2]—have indeed signaled the change, but their voices have been largely unheeded.

One reason is the deceptive acceleration of exponential growth. With a constant rate of growth, the world will go from half-full to totally full in one doubling period—the same amount of time that it took to go from 1 percent full to 2 percent. Of course, the doubling time itself has shortened, compounding the deceptive acceleration. If we take the percent appropriation by human beings of the net product of land-based photosynthesis as an index of how full the world is of humans and their furniture, then we can say that it is 40 percent full because we use, directly and indirectly, about 40 percent of the net primary product of land-based photosynthesis.[3] Taking thirty-five years as the doubling time of the human scale (that is, population times per capita resource use) and calculating backward, we go from the present 40 percent to only 10 percent full in just two doubling times, or seventy years, which is about an average lifetime. Also, "full" here is taken as 100 percent human appropriation of the net product of photosynthesis, which on the face of it would seem to be ecologically quite unlikely and socially undesirable (only the most recalcitrant species would remain wild—all others would be managed for human benefit). In other words, effective fullness occurs at less than 100 percent human preemption of net photosynthetic product, and there is much evidence that long-run human carrying capacity is reached at less than the existing 40 percent (see Chapter 1). The world has rapidly gone from relatively empty (10 percent full) to relatively full (40 percent full). Although 40 percent is less than half, it makes sense to think of it as indicating relative fullness because it is only one doubling time away from 80 percent, a figure that represents excessive fullness. This change has been faster than the speed with which fundamental economic paradigms shift. According to physicist Max Planck, a new scientific paradigm triumphs not by convincing the majority of its opponents, but because its opponents eventually die. There has not yet been time for the empty-world economists to die, and meanwhile they have been cloning themselves faster than they are dying by maintaining tight control over their guild. The disciplinary structure of knowledge in modern economics is far tighter than that of the turn-of-the-century physics that was Planck's model. Full-world economics is not yet accepted as academically legitimate; indeed it is not even recognized as a challenge.[4]

Another reason for failing to note the watershed change in the pattern of scarcity is that in order to speak of a *limiting* factor, the factors must be thought of as complementary. If factors are good substitutes, then a shortage of one does not significantly limit the productivity of the other. A standard assumption of neoclassical economics has been that factors of production are highly substitutable. Although other models of production have considered factors as not at all substitutable (for example, the total complementarity of the Leontief model), the substitutability assumption has dominated. Consequently the very idea of a limiting factor was pushed into the background. If factors are substitutes rather than complements, then there can be no limiting factor and hence no new era based on a change of the limiting role from one factor to another. It is therefore important to be very clear on the issue of complementarity versus substitutability.[5]

The productivity of manmade capital is more and more limited by the decreasing supply of complementary natural capital. Of course in the past, when the scale of the human presence in the biosphere was low, manmade capital played the limiting role. The switch from manmade to natural capital as the limiting factor is thus a function of the increasing scale and impact of the human presence. Natural capital is the stock that yields the flow of natural resources—the forest that yields the flow of cut timber; the petroleum deposits that yield the flow of pumped crude oil; the fish populations in the sea that yield the flow of caught fish. The complementary nature of natural and manmade capital is made obvious by asking, what good is a saw mill without a forest? a refinery without petroleum deposits? a fishing boat without populations of fish? Beyond some point in the accumulation of manmade capital it is clear that the limiting factor on production will be remaining natural capital. For example, the limiting factor determining the fish catch is the reproductive capacity of fish populations, not the number of fishing boats; for gasoline the limiting factor is petroleum deposits, not refinery capacity; and for many types of wood it is remaining forests, not saw mill capacity. Costa Rica and peninsular Malaysia, for example, now must import logs to keep their saw mills employed. One country can accumulate manmade capital and deplete natural capital to a greater extent only if another country does it to a lesser extent—for example, Costa Rica must import logs from somewhere. The demands of complementarity between manmade and natural capital can be evaded within a nation only if they are respected between nations.

Of course, multiplying specific examples of complementarity between natural and manmade capital will never suffice to prove the general case. But the examples given above at least serve to add concreteness to the more general arguments for the complementarity hypothesis given in the next section.

Because of the complementary relation between manmade and natural capital, the very accumulation of manmade capital puts pressure on natural capital stocks to supply an increasing flow of natural resources. When that flow reaches a size that can no longer be maintained, there is a big temptation to supply the annual flow unsustainably by liquidation of natural capital stocks, thus postponing the collapse in the value of the complementary manmade capital. Indeed, in the era of empty-world economics, natural resources and natural capital were considered free goods (except for extraction or harvest costs). Consequently the value of manmade capital was under no threat from scarcity of a complementary factor. In the era of full-world economics, this threat is real and is met by liquidating stocks of natural capital to temporarily keep up the flow of natural resources that support the value of manmade capital. Hence the problem of sustainability.

More on Complementarity Versus Substitutability

The main issue is the relation between natural capital, which yields a flow of natural resources and services that enter the process of production, and the manmade capital that serves as an agent in the process for transforming the resource inflow into a product outflow. Is the flow of natural resources (and the stock of natural capital that yields that flow) substitutable by manmade capital? Clearly, one resource can substitute for another—we can transform aluminum instead of copper into electric wire, for example. We can also substitute labor for capital, or capital for labor, to a significant degree, even though the characteristic of complementarity is also important. For example, we can have fewer carpenters and more power saws, or fewer power saws and more carpenters, and still build the same house. But more pilots cannot substitute for fewer airplanes, once the airplanes are fully employed. In other words, one resource can substitute for another, albeit imperfectly, because both play the same qualitative role in production—both are raw materials undergoing transformation into a product. Likewise capital and labor are substitutable to a significant degree because both play the role of agent of transformation of resource inputs into product outputs. However, when we come to substitution across the roles of transforming agent and material undergoing transformation (efficient cause and material cause), the possibilities of substitution become very limited, and the characteristic of complementarity is dominant. For example, we cannot make the same house with half the lumber no matter how many extra power saws or carpenters we try to substitute. Of course, we might substitute brick for lumber, but then we face the analogous limitation—we cannot substitute masons and trowels for bricks.

The Complementarity of Natural and Manmade Capital

The upshot of these considerations is that natural capital (natural resources) and manmade capital are complements rather than substitutes. The neoclassical assumption of near perfect substitutability between natural resources and manmade capital is a serious distortion of reality, the excuse of "analytical convenience" notwithstanding. To see how serious, imagine that in fact manmade capital were indeed a perfect substitute for natural resources. Then it would also be the case that natural resources would be a perfect substitute for manmade capital.

Yet if that were so, we would have had no reason whatsoever to accumulate manmade capital, since we were already endowed by nature with a perfect substitute! Historically, of course, we did accumulate manmade capital long before natural capital was depleted, precisely because we needed manmade capital to make effective use of the natural capital (complementarity!). It is quite amazing that the substitutability dogma should be held with such tenacity in the face of such an easy *reductio ad absurdum*. Add to that the fact that capital itself requires natural resources for its production—that is, the substitute itself requires the very input being substituted for—and it is quite clear that manmade capital and natural resources are fundamentally complements, not substitutes. Substitutability of capital for resources is limited to reducing waste of materials in process—for example, collecting sawdust and using a press (capital) to make particle board. And no amount of substitution of capital for resources can ever reduce the mass of material resource inputs below the mass of the outputs, given the law of conservation of matter-energy.

Substitutability of capital for resources in aggregate-production functions reflects largely a change in the total product mix from resource-intensive to different capital-intensive products. It is an artifact of product aggregation, not factor substitution—that is, along a given product isoquant. It is important to emphasize that it is this latter meaning of substitution—producing a given physical product with fewer natural resources and more capital—that is under attack here. No one denies that it is possible to produce a different product or a different product mix with fewer resources. Indeed, new products may be designed to provide the same or better service while using fewer resources, and sometimes less labor and less capital as well. This is technical improvement, not substitution of capital for resources. Light bulbs that give more lumens per watt represent technical progress, qualitative improvement in the state of the arts, not the substitution of a quantity of capital for a quantity of natural resource in the production of a given quantity of a product.

It may be that economists are speaking loosely and metaphorically when they claim that capital is a near perfect substitute for natural resources. Perhaps they are counting as "capital" all improvements in knowledge, technology, managerial skill, etc.—in short, anything that would increase the efficiency with which resources are used. If this is the usage, then "capital" and resources would by definition be substitutes in the same sense that more efficient use of a resource is a substitute for using more of the resource. But to define capital as efficiency would make a mockery of the neoclassical theory of production, where efficiency is a ratio of output to input, and capital is a quantity of input.

The productivity of manmade capital is more and more limited by the decreasing supply of complementary natural capital. In the past, when the scale of the human presence in the biosphere was low, manmade capital played the limiting role. The switch from manmade to natural capital as the limiting factor is thus a function of the increasing scale of the human presence.

More on Natural Capital

Thinking of the natural environment as "natural capital" is in some ways unsatisfactory, but useful within limits. We may define capital broadly as a stock of something that yields a flow of useful goods or services. Traditionally capital was defined as produced means of production, which we are here calling manmade capital as distinct from natural capital, which, though not made by man, is nevertheless functionally a stock that yields a flow of useful goods and services. We can distinguish renewable from nonrenewable, and marketed from nonmarketed, natural capital, giving four cross-categories. Pricing natural capital, especially nonmarketable natural capital, is so far an intractable problem, but one that need not be faced here. All that need be recognized for the argument at hand is that natural capital consists of physical stocks that are complementary to manmade capital. We have learned to use the concept of human capital (acquired skills and knowledge), which departs even more fundamentally from the standard definition of capital. Human capital cannot be bought and sold, although it can be rented. Although it can be accumulated, it cannot be inherited without effort by bequest as can ordinary manmade capital, but must be relearned anew by each generation. Natural capital, however, is more like traditional manmade capital in that it can be bequeathed. Overall, the concept of natural capital is less a departure from the traditional definition of capital than is the commonly used notion of human capital.

There is a troublesome subcategory of marketed natural capital that is intermediate between natural and manmade, which we might refer to as "cultivated natural capital," consisting of such things as plantation forests, herds of livestock, agricultural crops, fish bred in ponds, etc. Cultivated natural capital supplies the raw material input complementary to manmade capital, but it does not provide the wide range of natural ecological services characteristic of natural capital proper. For example, eucalyptus plantations supply timber to saw mills and may even reduce erosion, but do not provide wildlife habitat nor preserve biodiversity. Investment in the cultivated natural capital of plantation forests, however, is useful not only for the lumber, but as a way of easing the pressure of lumber interests on the remaining true natural capital of real forests.

Marketed natural capital can, subject to the important social corrections for common property and myopic discounting, be left to the market. Nonmarketed natural capital, both renewable and nonrenewable, will be the most troublesome category. Remaining natural forests should in many cases be treated as nonmarketed natural capital, and only replanted areas treated as marketed natural capital. In neoclassical terms, the external benefits of remaining natural forests might be considered "infinite," thus removing them from market competition with other (inferior) uses. Most neoclassical economists, however, have a strong aversion to any imputation of an "infinite" or prohibitive price to anything.

Policy Implications of the Turning Point

In this new full-world era, investment must shift from manmade capital accumulation toward natural capital preservation and restoration. Also technology should be aimed at increasing the productivity of natural capital more than manmade capital. If these two things do not happen, we will be behaving *uneconomically*—in the most orthodox sense of the word. That is, the emphasis should shift from technologies that increase the productivity of labor and manmade capital to those that increase the productivity of natural capital. This would occur by market forces if the price of natural capital were to rise as it became more scarce. What keeps the price from rising? In most cases natural capital is unowned and consequently nonmarketed. Therefore it has no explicit price and is exploited as if its price were zero. Even where prices exist on natural capital the market tends to be myopic and excessively discounts the costs of future scarcity, especially when under the influence of economists who teach that accumulating capital is a near perfect substitute for depleting natural resources!

Natural capital productivity is increased by: (1) increasing the flow (net growth) of natural resources per unit of natural stock (limited by biological growth rates); (2) increasing product output per unit of resource input (limited by mass balance); and especially by (3) increasing the end-use efficiency with which the resulting product yields services to the final user (limited by technology). We have already argued that complementarity severely limits what we should expect from (2), and complex ecological interrelations and the law of conservation of matter-energy will limit the increase from (1). Therefore the focus should be mainly on (3).

The above factors limit productivity from the supply side. From the demand side, tastes may provide a limit to the economic productivity of natural capital that is more stringent than the limit of biological productivity. For example, game ranching and fruit gathering in a natural tropical forest may, in terms of biomass, be more productive than cattle ranching. But undeveloped tastes for game meat and tropical fruit may make this use less profitable than the biologically less productive use of cattle ranching. In this case a change in tastes can increase the biological productivity with which the land is used.

Since manmade capital is owned by the capitalist, we can expect that it will be maintained with an interest to increasing its productivity. Labor power, which is a stock that yields the useful services of labor, can be treated in the same way as manmade capital. Labor power is manmade and owned by the laborer, who has an interest in maintaining it and enhancing its productivity. But nonmarketed natural capital (the water cycle, the ozone layer, the atmosphere, etc.) is not subject to ownership, and no self-interested social class can be relied upon to protect it from overexploitation.

If the thesis argued above were accepted by development economists and the multilateral development banks, what policy implications would follow? The role of the multilateral development banks in the new era would be increasingly to make investments that replenish the stock and increase the productivity of natural capital. In the past, development investments have largely aimed at increasing the stock and productivity of manmade capital. Instead of investing mainly in saw mills, fishing boats, and refineries, development banks should now invest more in reforestation, restocking of fish populations, and renewable substitutes for dwindling petroleum reserves. The latter should include investment in energy efficiency, since it is impossible to restock petroleum deposits. Since natural capacity to absorb wastes is also a vital resource, investments that preserve that capacity (for example, pollution reduction) also increase in priority. For marketed natural capital this will not represent a revolutionary change. For nonmarketed natural capital it will be more difficult, but even here economic development agencies have experience in investing in complementary public goods such as education, legal systems, public infrastructure, and population control. Investments in limiting the rate of growth of the human population are of greatest importance in managing a world that has become relatively full. Like manmade capital, manmade labor power is also complementary with natural resources, and its growth can increase demand for natural resources beyond the capacity of natural capital to sustainably supply.

Perhaps the clearest policy implication of the full-world thesis is that the level of per capita resource use of the rich countries cannot be generalized to the poor, given the current world population. Present total resource use levels are already unsustainable, and multiplying them by a factor of five to ten as envisaged in the Brundtland Report, albeit with considerable qualification, is ecologically impossible. As a policy of growth becomes less possible, the importance of redistribution and population control as measures to combat poverty increase correspondingly. In a full world both human numbers and per capita resource use must be constrained. Poor countries cannot cut per capita resource use; indeed they must increase it to reach a sufficiency, so their focus must be mainly on population control. Rich countries can cut both, and for those that have already reached demographic equilibrium, the focus would be more on limiting per capita consumption to make resources available for transfer to help bring the poor up to sufficiency. Investments in population control and redistribution therefore increase in priority for development agencies.

Investing in natural capital (nonmarketed) is essentially an infrastructure investment on a grand scale and in the most fundamental sense of infrastructure—that is, the biophysical infrastructure of the entire human niche, not just the within-niche public investments that support the productivity of the private investments. Rather we are now talking about investments in biophysical infrastructure ("infra-infrastructure") to maintain the productivity of all previous economic investments in manmade capital, be they public or private, by investing in rebuilding the remaining natural capital stocks, which have come to be limitative. Indeed, in the new era the World Bank's official name, the International Bank for Reconstruction and Development, should emphasize the word *reconstruction* and redefine it to mean reconstruction of natural capital devastated by rapacious "development," as opposed to the historical meaning of reconstruction of manmade capital in Europe devastated by World War II. Since our ability to recreate natural capital is very limited, such investments will have to be indirect—that is, conserve the remaining natural capital and encourage its natural growth by reducing our level of current exploitation. This includes investing in projects that relieve the pressure on these natural capital stocks by expanding cultivated natural capital (plantation forests to relieve pressure on natural forests, for example) and by increasing end-use efficiency of products.

The difficulty with infrastructure investments is that their productivity shows up in the enhanced return on other investments and is therefore difficult both to calculate and to collect for loan repayment. Also, in the present context, these ecological infrastructure investments are defensive and restorative in nature—that is, they will protect existing rates of return from falling more rapidly than otherwise, rather than raising their rate of return to a higher level. This circumstance will dampen the political enthusiasm for such investments but will not alter the economic logic favoring them. Past high rates of return on manmade capital were possible only with unsustainable rates of use of natural resources and consequent (uncounted) liquidation of natural capital. We are now learning to deduct natural capital liquidation from our measure of national income.[6] The new era of sustainable development will not permit natural capital liquidation to count as income and will consequently require that we become accustomed to lower rates of return on manmade capital—rates on the order of magnitude of the biological growth rates of natural capital, since that will be the limiting factor. Once investments in natural capital have resulted in equilibrium stocks that are maintained but not expanded (yielding a constant total resource flow), then all further increase in economic welfare would have to come from increases in pure efficiency resulting from improvements in technology and clarification of priorities. Certainly investments are being made in increasing biological growth rates, and the advent of genetic engineering will add greatly to this thrust. However, experience to date (for example, the green revolution) indicates that higher biological yield rates usually require the sacrifice of some other useful quality (disease resistance, flavor, strength of stalk). In any case, the law of conservation of matter-energy cannot be evaded by genetics: more food from a plant or animal implies either more inputs or less matter-energy going to the nonfood structures and functions of the organism. To avoid ecological backlashes will require leadership and clarity of purpose on the part of development agencies. To carry the arguments for infrastructure investments into the area of biophysical/ environmental infrastructure or natural capital replenishment will require new thinking by development economists. Since much natural capital is not only public but globally public in nature, the United Nations seems indicated to take a leadership role.

Consider two specific cases of biospheric infrastructure investments and the difficulties they present. (1) A largely deforested country will need reforestation to keep the complementary manmade capital of saw mills (carpentry, cabinetry skills, etc.) from losing their value. Of course, for a time, the deforested country could resort to importing logs. To protect the manmade capital of dams from the silting of the lakes behind them, the water catchment areas feeding the lakes must be reforested or the original forests protected to prevent erosion and siltation. Agricultural investments depending on irrigation can become worthless without forested water catchment areas that recharge aquifers. (2) At a global level, enormous stocks of manmade capital and natural capital are threatened by depletion of the ozone layer, although the exact consequences are too uncertain to be predicted. The greenhouse effect is a threat to the value of all coastally located and climatically dependent capital, be it manmade (port cities, wharves, beach resorts) or natural (estuarine breeding grounds for fish and shrimp). And if the natural capital of fish populations diminishes due to loss of breeding grounds, then the value of the manmade capital of fishing boats and canneries will also be diminished in value, as will the specialized human capital devoted to fishing, canning, etc. We have begun to adjust national accounts for the liquidation of natural capital, but have not yet recognized that the value of complementary manmade capital must also be written down as the natural capital that it was designed to exploit disappears. Eventually the market will automatically lower the valuation of fishing boats as fish disappear, so perhaps no accounting adjustments are called for. But ex ante policy adjustments aimed at avoiding the ex post writing down of complementary manmade capital, whether by market or accountant, is certainly called for.

Initial Policy Response to the Turning Point

Although there is as yet no indication of the degree to which development economists would agree with the fundamental thesis here argued, three United National agencies (World Bank, United Nations Environment Program, and United National Development Program) have nevertheless embarked on a project, however exploratory and modest, of biospheric infrastructure investment known as the Global Environment Facility. The Facility would provide concessional funding for programs investing in the preservation or enhancement of four classes of biospheric infrastructure of nonmarketed natural capital. These are: protection of the ozone layer, reduction of greenhouse gas emissions, protection of international water resources, and protection of biodiversity. If the thesis argued here is correct, then investments of this type should eventually become very important in the lending portfolios of development banks. Likewise the thesis would provide theoretical justification and guidance for present efforts to found the Global Environment Facility and its likely extensions. It would seem that the "new era" thesis merits serious discussion, both inside and outside the multilateral development banks, especially since it appears that our practical policy response to the reality of the new era has already outrun our theoretical understanding of it.

Acknowledgments

I am grateful to P. Ehrlich, B. Hannon, G. Lozada, R. Overby, S. Postel, B. von Droste, and P. Dogsé for helpful comments.

Notes

1. K. Boulding, *The Meaning of the Twentieth Century* (New York: Harper and Row, 1964).

2. N. Georgescu-Roegen, *The Entropy Law and the Economic Process* (Cambridge: Harvard University Press, 1971).

3. P. M. Vitousek et al., "Human Appropriation of the Products of Photosynthesis," *BioScience* 34(6)(1986): 368–73.

4. For an analysis of economics as an academic discipline, see Part I of H. E. Daly and J. B. Cobb, *For the Common Good: Redirecting the Economy Toward Community, Environment, and a Sustainable Future* (Boston: Beacon Press, 1989).

5. The usual Hicks-Allen definition of complementarity and substitutability is: "If a rise in the j th factor price, which reduces the use of the j th factor, increases (resp. reduces) the use of the i th factor for each fixed [level of output],

i is a substitute (resp. complement) for j." [From A. Takayama, *Mathematical Economics*, 2d ed. (New York: Cambridge University Press, 1985), 144.] In a model with only two factors, it follows from this definition that the factors *must* be substitutes. If they were complements, then a rise in the price of one of them would reduce the use of both factors while output remained constant, which is impossible. The customary diagrammatic use of two-factor models thus reinforces the focus on substitutability by effectively defining complementarity out of existence in the two-factor case. In the Leontief model of L-shaped isoquants (fixed coefficients), the above definition simply breaks down because the reduction in use of one factor inevitably causes a reduction in output, which the definition requires must remain constant. For the argument of this paper, one need appeal only to "complementarity" in the sense of a limiting factor. A factor becomes limiting when an increase in the other factor(s) will not increase output, but an increase in the factor in question (the limiting factor) will increase output. For a limiting factor, all that is needed is that the isoquant become parallel to one of the axes. And for the practical argument of this paper, "nearly parallel" would also be quite sufficient.

6. Y. Ahmad, S. El Serafy, and E. Lutz, eds., *Environmental Accounting for Sustainable Development* (Washington, D.C.: World Bank, 1989).

3

On the Strategy of Trying to Reduce Economic Inequality by Expanding the Scale of Human Activity

Trygve Haavelmo and Stein Hansen

The Big Dilemma

Sustainable development as advocated in the Brundtland Report[1] requires a rate of global economic growth and a distribution of assets and income that would allow developing countries to achieve a significant per capita increase in disposable income as a basis for achieving alleviation of poverty. Invariably, policy statements to this effect mean a strategy whereby the standards of the poor shall be lifted toward the level of the well-to-do and to the forms of consumption and investments seen in the industrialized countries today.

Such policy statements appear to be founded on a belief that there are, and will be in the future of concern to society, no serious limits to material growth. The various factors of production—natural resources, manmade capital, and labor—are assumed to be substitutable so that a shortage of one does not significantly limit the productivity of another.

At the same time, the World Commission on Environment and Development (WCED) expresses serious concern about the global consequences of human activity in the way of pollution, exhaustion of resources, and generally the danger of deteriorating the environment for future generations to live in. Such concerns appear to reflect the belief that there are, and will increasingly be, serious limits to growth—that is, some of the key factors of production are complementary rather than substitutable.

More specifically, as Herman Daly has put it (see Chapter 2), the concern expresses a suspicion that an ever-increasing flow of input of natural resources in the production processes to sustain the required growth inevitably results in liquidating of the natural capital stock that supplies this flow. Manmade capital is created from inputs of labor and natural capital and serves as an agent along with labor in the process of transforming the resource flow into utility-yielding output flow. If this very resource flow is reduced or disappears, the productivity of the transformation agents—manmade capital and labor—is reduced. For example, what is the value of a saw mill without a forest to supply logs, or fishing boats without a fish population to catch? Thus complementarity rather than substitutability between the flow of natural resources on the one hand, and manmade capital on the other, must be recognized as a clear possibility and considered for inclusion as a fundamental assumption for economic planning. This implies that the very accumulation of manmade capital puts increasing pressure on natural capital stocks to supply an increasing flow of natural resources to sustain the productivity of manmade capital.

The case of natural resource cultivation such as farming illustrates this. Agriculturists established long ago that the basic principle of farming is to change the local natural system into one that produces more of the goods desired by man. This manmade system is an artificial construction that requires continuous economic inputs obtained from the natural environment to maintain its output level. Much of the farming input is thus an effort to prevent the established artificial state of the land from declining toward an unproductive (from a human perspective) low-level state, most likely lower than the natural state prior to farming of the land.[2]

Fundamentally, rearrangement of matter is the central physical fact about the economic process. Matter cannot be destroyed in the economic system; it can merely be converted or dissipated. These transformation processes generate wastes—some that can be economically recycled and some that cannot. To the extent that nature's capacity to assimilate such wastes is or becomes inadequate, wastes will accumulate. Energy is degraded in these transformations. This means that little by little the capacity to rearrange matter is irrevocably used up. Energy flows also drive the basic physical, chemical, and biological life-support systems: air, water, and soils. It is eventually the capacity of these systems that will limit the scale of human activity—that is, long-term global economic growth.[3]

Sustainable development implies a perspective of several generations or centuries. Clearly, development where population and per capita use of the planet's finite resources both grow significantly cannot go on indefinitely. Even if population and the level of economic activity were kept stationary, accumulation of pollutants would grow very rapidly because of the growth of entropy beyond nature's capacity for self-repair. Entropy is a concept borrowed, somewhat freely, from physics. The concept as used here can be defined as an index measuring the total accumulation of useless or harmful wastes produced by human activities over a relevant span of recent economic history.[4]

The politically widely acclaimed WCED definition of sustainable development invariably implies lifting the bottom rather than lowering the top. Successful achievement of global equity goals via growth and economic efficiency, as conventionally measured in the national income accounts, will contradict the environmental dimensions of sustainable development.[5] Even the sturdiest ship will eventually sink if the load is too big. There is little comfort in the fact that the load was optimally allocated and fairly distributed at the time of sinking.[6]

To make political difficulties worse, even with wide acceptance that lowering the top is required, continued accumulative strain on the natural resource base would be the likely outcome, albeit at a reduced rate. The development process has a tremendous momentum. It can be likened to a journey: You start out from Manila and your destination is Bali. Instead, you head north toward Tokyo. You realize that the direction of travel will not take you to Bali. Therefore, you reduce traveling speed—you slow down—but you do not change the direction of travel. While this will postpone your time of arrival in Tokyo, it will not take you any closer to Bali.[7]

The Technological Optimistic View

History is full of technological pessimists. The economists of the nineteenth century saw the natural resource base as a limiting factor that would eventually drive the productivity of the transformative agents—labor and capital—down to a level corresponding to a subsistence standard of living.[8] Some of them predicted that the Industrial Revolution would end as coal mines were exhausted. Most doomsayers did not foresee the ability of society, through human capital formation and organization of societies, to improve manmade capital so as to facilitate an unprecedented rate of natural resource extraction to meet rapidly increasing and diversifying consumer demands, thus yielding very attractive returns on manmade capital and labor in many societies.

Many people today look upon those who warn against pollution and exhaustion of resources as technological pessimists. On the other hand, technological optimism is based on a faith in scientific development and technological progress.

Thoughts from the field of decisions under uncertainty also enter the picture. There is the question of who has the burden of proof—the optimist or the pessimist? Here we find two extreme views. One is that since we do not know for certain that the future will be difficult, why worry? The other view is that we should be concerned about the future because we cannot be sure that the future will not be difficult. Both views risk making wrong predictions. Even if we could estimate the chances of right or wrong predictions, there is the question of which mistake is the more serious. Here there is a strong degree of asymmetry. The irreversible effects of an "optimist's" reckless policy are likely to be vastly more difficult to cope with than the outcome of a more cautious "pessimist's" policy.[9]

Technological development—which is qualitative progress and thus fundamentally different from quantitative substitution of manmade capital for natural resources (see Chapter 2)—could take place along two lines relevant to the issues at stake here. The one line is improvement in the ability to utilize available resources at any time to produce more and more goods. The other line reduces the negative effects of growing entropy. Possibly technological ability in the methods of producing wanted goods and services could develop faster than the negative effects of growing entropy. Even if the negative effects of entropy kept increasing, conceivably people in the future would prefer twice as many goods as we have today, even if they had to wear gas masks. It is even possible that human tastes and preferences would gradually develop in this direction. But there is a fundamental flaw in this "optimistic" line of reasoning.

If the development of the production of goods and services has reached a certain level at which entropy grows in spite of cleaning efforts, further development of the ability to produce goods and services has to go on increasing. If the ability to produce goods and services should level off at a higher level, it is just a question of time for the negative effects of entropy to catch up with development. In other words, one would have to produce goods and services at a steadily increasing rate in order to stave off the growing effects of entropy that would creep up as time goes on.[10] Even worse, lowering entropy of the economic subsystem requires increasing entropy of the rest of the system (the environment). Since "the rest of the system" includes the sun, the inevitable entropy increase can be charged to the solar account, but only for a solar-based economy, not a fossil-fuel-based economy.[11]

If we could be sure that this eternal chase is according to the informed preferences of society, there is, of course, not much to be added. The sacred status of consumer sovereignty is the key in this connection. But to what extent do people know what they are doing in the long run? Or, more profoundly, to what extent is it possible at all for people as individuals to make the choice of their future path of development?[12]

The Free Market Principle Will Not Provide the Answer

As is well known, the free market mechanism with equilibrium prices has certain optimal properties. But there are many assumptions that have to be fulfilled in order to ensure these properties. A fundamental assumption is that there be no collective (or external) side effects of production or consumption, in addition to what individuals consider as the immediate product of interest to them. *If collective side effects (externalities) are substantial and important, the classical doctrine of the blessings of free trade simply becomes irrelevant as a guideline for economic policy.* This is a conclusion that any serious student of economics can verify by means of standard economic textbook theory.

There are three kinds of side effects of a collective nature that are important in the present context: (1) the production of immediate pollution in the process of production, or production pollution; (2) the indirect effects of the pollution produced by consumers as a by-product of their enjoying goods and services they buy, or consumption pollution; and (3) the negative effects of entropy and its impact on environmental deterioration, or environmental pollution.

Every day we hear complaints from producers that their business would not be profitable were they to pay for the pollution and environmental deterioration that they cause. We observe a rapidly growing market for shipping toxic, carcinogenic, and other waste materials from production and consumption in industrialized countries to developing countries for dumping or recycling. There the laws and regulations on handling, recycling, dumping, and storage are often more lenient than those in industrialized economies, where the negative hazards and crowding effects of the accumulating undesirable waste are becoming too costly for comfort.

Consumers are led to overestimate the value of the goods and services they buy because they take the "surrounding," or natural environment, as something given free in any case. This was already well known from the writings of Pigou.[13] In addition to all this comes the human weakness of preferring present goods to future goods, as was pointed out long ago by von Boehm-Bawerk.[14]

These factors illustrate the difficulty of relying on individual action in making a wise choice from the point of view of the distant future. It is extremely difficult to modify a free market system by means of taxes and subsidies in order to take care of all those side effects not included in the simple free market framework. Recent economic history is full of illustrations of how it has been found necessary to restrict the private market forces by publicly invoked constraints.

The core message from these considerations can be further strengthened by addressing the very important current problem in many countries of providing employment for their labor forces. Here the real economic problem has been turned almost upside-down. The idea of regular and "respectable" employment among employees is one of working and receiving income from employers who can pay the wages because what they produce can be sold profitably in the market. Individual employees cannot make it their business to decide whether or not what they produce is desirable from a global point of view. According to the principle of consumer sovereignty, if there is a market for what the employee helps to produce, then somebody must prefer the product. Hence it is a good thing. Whatever side effects employees simultaneously help to produce (for example, environmental damage), they cannot be blamed for, because their partial influence on such side effects is infinitesimal as compared to their immediate gain from their work and income.

Will Technological Advances Benefit the Strong or the Weak?

Two conflicting developments can be conceived of in response to such a question. The first possibility is that advances in technological skill and know-how will benefit the strong relatively more than the weak. If the strong (like other people) are primarily selfish, the outcome may be a widening of the inequality in the world. This tendency is further exacerbated if those who develop technical advances focus on consumer goods and services for a high level of living, rather than focusing on more elementary improvements of using the world's resources to benefit the poor.

Second, however, is the possibility that increasing ability to utilize resources more effectively and reduce pollution could be used to help those who are less fortunate and less able to take care of themselves. The disputed "trickle down" theory could perhaps lead to such an outcome even with the strong being primarily selfish. However, it is beyond economic theory to speculate on the final conclusion as to what might be the outcome of such conflicting tendencies.

What Kind of North-South Trade and Aid Cooperation?

Governments and individuals have for decades assumed natural re-source inputs to be abundant, whereas manmade capital and skilled labor needed to transform the natural resources into useful consumption and investment goods have been considered the scarce factors. A consequence of such perceptions and their penetration into commodity market formation has been the falling relative raw materials prices in world markets. This has contributed to a widening of the North-South gap between industrialized and many natural-resource-dependent developing countries.

Such deterioration has been further intensified as a consequence of the global trend-setting production and consumption patterns of rich countries. Poor countries are tempted to exhaust their own valuable natural resource stocks at low prices in return for imported machinery and consumer goods. Export is not an end in itself. Export only serves a purpose if it can finance useful imports. Developing countries should realize they must stringently avoid exports they cannot afford. Strategies to enhance exports of many staple agricultural products should be critically revisited. Such goods face low demand elasticities in world markets. Individually, each exporter takes the world market price as given. In the aggregate, however, the simultaneous implementation of such strategies by many drives the price down dramatically as they all reach their production targets. In the end, the export revenue might fall short of paying for the imported machinery, implements, pesticides, etc., required to produce for export. The outcome is financial crisis and reduced capability to service increased debt burdens. Such trade includes not only sale of nonrenewable minerals and harvests from soils, forests, and oceans, but an increasing use of poor countries' soils as dumps and recycling sites for undesirable waste from industrial production and consumption.

While many positive things can be said about liberalizing and thus increasing trade, the structure of trade, as we know it at present, is a curse from the perspective of sustainable development.[15] A drive for efficient resource use in the presence of significant environmental externalities and other market imperfections requires full-cost pricing of resources in all applications. This in turn implies a need for substantial intervention at national and supranational levels into otherwise free market forces of domestic and international trade. Otherwise, countries that practice full-cost internalization would, in the short run, lose out to countries that did not, in a regime of free trade.

Poor countries should begin to realize the approaching scarcity of some of their natural resources and plan the exploitation of these accordingly. International and national policies pursued in a complex world of conflicting individual and group demands must come to grips with impending natural resource constraints. The global production structure is rapidly approaching a situation where the relative scarcity of input factors is about to be turned upside-down. Increasingly, it is the sustainable flows from natural resource stocks that are becoming the limiting production factors, not manmade capital and skilled labor (see Chapter 2).

This is clearly indicated by the rapid emergence of the technologically advanced "intermediate" input category that could be labeled cultivated natural capital—that is, "green revolution" agriculture, hybrid plantation forests, fish farming, etc. However, such high-efficiency artificial natural resources may lack the robust biodiversity dimensions of indigenous natural resources. While being intermediate between natural and manmade inputs, they are therefore far from perfect longrun substitutes for indigenous natural resources and are, in fact, subject to the growth of entropy constraints on economic development identified as a key growth dilemma earlier in this chapter.

This emerging new bargaining position is what the poor countries need to prepare for while they still have something with which to bargain. This requires preparation of development plans and programs for what the countries' economic activities should look like in the long run. Structural and sectoral adjustments, including changes in domestic price policies, and international debt management will be important components of plans for sustainable development.[16]

Aid cooperation with the purpose of assisting poor countries in a development toward the same pattern of polluting consumerism as the North has brought about is no contribution toward sustainable development. It will result in continued rent transfer from natural-resource-endowed developing countries to rich countries supplying the South with machinery for speedier resource extraction, which will result in keeping down their prices of natural resources.

On the other hand, aid cooperation with the purpose of assisting in the development of location-specific technologies and patterns of consumption adapted to local, cultural, and habitual patterns in order to enhance human development and quality of life in a sustainable way should be strongly endorsed.

Such assistance could serve as an eye-opener to the rich donors, thus helping them in the process toward a sustainable world as well. One possible way to operationalize the concept of sustainable development in economic planning and aid cooperation is by means of so-called compensatory investments.[17]

Already, some power companies in industrialized countries have decided that their long-term prospects will benefit from undertaking measures to counter the environmental impact from increased carbon dioxide emission. Tree planting at home or in another country, or installation of more energy-efficient devices in poor countries where the costs of reducing emissions are well below those at home, are real-world examples. One could foresee virgin tropical forests take on increased financial value to the owners if leased out to preserve biodiversity, to provide a natural and sustainable habitat for indigenous people, or to prevent a reduction in the global carbon sink capacity. This maximum sustainable income would be higher than the present worth of the combined financial returns to the owners from first cutting and exporting the logs, and then raising cattle for a few years, before the soils become exhausted. With self-imposed national emission barriers in rich countries, such opportunities could soon provide for new financially and economically sound trade and aid flows. The required institutional changes may be moderate.[18]

The Outlook: Is There a Solution?

No matter how people go about managing this earth and the life on it, there is always a "solution." Imagine some entity outside our planet that keeps some sort of record of what mankind does on Earth and the consequences of it. The development record might read like something out of Charles Darwin. That is, development might lead to some ecological balance as far as mankind is concerned, including the catastrophe (from mankind's perspective) that mankind becomes extinct.

What people mean by asking for a solution is presumably something else. This "something else" is presumably the following. Certain developments are, from the human perspective, more desirable than others. The human mind, being rational, is supposed to be able to make a sensible choice between various feasible alternatives when it comes to development. So the question boils down to this: Is there a "good" solution, or a solution that is acceptable?

At least three formidable conditions have to be fulfilled in order to get a positive answer to this question. The first is that we have a fairly good knowledge of the consequences of alternative paths of human activities in the future. Knowledge in this respect has probably made quite a bit of progress in recent years. The second condition is that there is an addressee or body to receive this knowledge and use it. The third condition is that this body or some other internationally accepted body be given the authority and power to choose the future path of development and enforce it.

About the last two conditions to be fulfilled we should have no illusions. Perhaps we should settle for the somewhat cynical answer suggested by some people—namely, that the situation on Earth as far as crowding, pollution, and deteriorated environments are concerned will not be recognized until the actual situation becomes much more precarious than is the case today.

This leads to what many might find paradoxical. Rapid growth and successful development as conventionally measured, combined with crowding and high population densities, could result in a menu of very few and very costly options for future development. In contrast, hitherto poor growth performance, low levels of infrastructure investments, slow utilization of the natural resource base, and a relatively sparse population (even if it is growing rapidly at present) could leave relatively more doors open in the choice of future developments.[19] Perhaps this is the flavor of optimism that could be presented for the peoples of Africa at this time of hardship.

The opportunities regarding possible actions for future sustainable development are limited and diminishing. It would not at all contribute toward sustainable development if nations continue to do as the bewildered tourist who in the treeless desert encountered a hungry lion. "But what did you do?" asked his friend afterward. "I climbed a tree," said the tourist. "But there were no trees around," said his friend. "Well, what else should I have done?" said the tourist.[20]

Conclusion

Policies for more equality invariably suggest that the standard of the poor be lifted toward the level of the rich—in other words, lifting the bottom rather than lowering the top. However, rapid growth and successful development as conventionally measured, combined with crowding and high population densities, could result in a menu of very few and costly options for future development. The opportunities regarding possible actions for future sustainable development are limited and diminishing. A "good" or acceptable development solution requires the fulfillment of at least three formidable conditions. The first is that we have a fairly good knowledge of the consequences of alternative paths of human activities in the future. The second is that there is an addressee to receive this knowledge and use it. The third is that this body or some other internationally accepted body be given the authority and power to choose the future path of development and enforce it. If these simple facts are not recognized, there is no more to be said about the sustainability issue or any other development policy.

Notes

1. World Commission on Environment and Development, "Our Common Future" (The Brundtland Report) (Oxford: Oxford University Press, 1987).

2. H. Ruthenberg, Farming Systems in the Tropics, 3d ed. (Oxford: Clarendon Press, 1980).

3. T. Haavelmo, "Forurensningrsproblemet fra et Samfunnsokonomisk Synspunkt" ("The Pollution Problem from a Global Perspective"), Sosialokonomen (Norwegian Journal of Economics), vol. 11, no. 4 (1971) (in Norwegian); Nicholas Georgescu-Roegen, The Entropy Law and the Economic Process (Cambridge: Harvard University Press, 1971).

4. T. Haavelmo, 1971, op. cit.

5. Asian Development Bank, Economic Policies for Sustainable Development (Manila: Asian Development Bank, 1990).

6. H. E. Daly and J. B. Cobb, For the Common Good: Redirecting the Economy Toward Community, the Environment, and a Sustainable Future (Boston: Beacon Press, 1989).

7. T. Haavelmo, "On the Dynamics of Global Economic Inequality," in Economic Policies for Sustainable Development, op. cit.

8. M. Blaug, Economic Theory in Retrospect (London: Heineman, 1962).

9. T. Haavelmo, A Study in the Theory of Economic Evolution (Amsterdam: North Holland Publishing Co. 1954); S. Hansen, "Naturvern eller Naturressurser" ("Natural Resources for Conservation or Economic Growth"), Sosialokonomen (Norwegian Journal of Economics), vol. 23, no. 2 (1969) (in Norwegian); T. Haavelmo, "Some Observations on Welfare and Economic Growth," in Induction, Growth and Trade: Essays in Honour of Sir Roy Harrod, ed. W. A. Eltis, M. F. G. Scott, and J. N. Wolfe (Oxford: Clarendon Press, 1970).

10. Haavelmo, 1971, op. cit.

11. Personal communication from H. E. Daly, 1991.

12. Haavelmo, 1954, 1970, and 1971, op. cit.

13. A. Pigou, The Economics of Welfare (London: Macmillan, 1920).

14. E. von Boehm-Bawerk, The Positive Theory of Capital (1891).

15. Asian Development Bank, 1990, op. cit., p. 7.

16. S. Hansen, "Debt for Nature Swaps: Overview and Discussion of Key Issues," Ecological Economics 1(1)(1989): 77–93; S. Hansen, "Macroeconomic Policies and Sustainable Development in the Third World," Journal of International Development 2(4)(1990): 533–57.

17. D. Pearce, A. Markandya, and E. Barbier, *Blueprint for a Green Economy* (London: Earthscan Publications, 1989).

18. P. Bohm, *Efficiency Issues and the Montreal Protocol on CFCs* (Environment Department Working Paper 40) (Washington, D.C.: World Bank, 1990).

19. Haavelmo, 1954, op. cit.

20. Asian Development Bank, 1990, op. cit., p. 7.

4

GNP and Market Prices: Wrong Signals for Sustainable Economic Success That Mask Environmental Destruction

Jan Tinbergen and Roefie Hueting

Society Is Steering by the Wrong Compass

The market is rightly considered a mechanism that generates man-made goods and services according to consumer preference. This mechanism allows culture and technology to put into practice inventions that enrich human life. It works efficiently and stimulates productivity increase, which is the motor raising the quantity, quality, and diversity of manmade goods thus becoming available to consumers.

An effective measure of the level of production and its changes from year to year—the national income—was devised in the 1930s (Tinbergen, quoted in Hueting 1980). People working on this research were well aware that national income would not form a complete indicator of economic success (welfare). But given a fair distribution of income and perfect competition, it no longer matters what is produced, only how much of it is produced. Consequently, at that time, great value was attached to the compilation of a series of figures on the total production of goods and services. In the 1930s, external effects such as environmental deterioration, did not yet play an important role.

This situation has changed drastically. During the last forty-five years, the period in which, based on the above reasoning, growth of

52

national income has been given the highest priority in economic policy, the following picture emerges.

The production of manmade goods and services has increased unprecedentedly, but has been accompanied by an unprecedented destruction of the most fundamental, scarce, and consequently economic good at human disposal—namely, the environment. This process has already caused much human suffering. Much of what are called natural disasters—such as erosion, flooding, and desertification—is caused by mismanagement of the environment. This process threatens the living conditions of generations to come. Furthermore, part of the growth of national income consists of production increases in arms, alcohol, tobacco, and drugs. Few people consider this progress. Part of the growth in gross national product (GNP) is double counting. Thus, environmental losses are not written off as costs, but expenditures for their partial recuperation or compensation *are* written up as final consumption. The same holds true for expenditures on victims of traffic accidents and diseases caused by consumption, such as smoking.

Increase in production is distributed very unequally. In rich countries, people are led to consume more because of seductive billion-dollar advertising. But 20 percent of the population in poor countries are deprived of basic needs, such as adequate food, shelter, potable water, taps, and toilets. Economic research has shown that once basic needs have been met, relative income has a greater impact on welfare than absolute income. Finally, production increase has not prevented the persistence of high unemployment worldwide and considerable child labor.

The market works well, but not all factors contributing to human welfare are captured by it. Consequently, market prices and economic indicators based on them, such as national income and cost-benefit analyses, misleadingly signal to society and therefore must be corrected. The factor for which correction is most urgently needed is the environment.

The Relationship Between Growth and Environmental Destruction

Environmental degradation is a consequence of production and its growth. The burden on the environment is determined by the number of people, the amount of activity per person, and the nature of that activity. These three factors are all reflected in the level of national income, albeit the number of people with a time lag (to be incorporated into the labor force). The increase and decrease of the first two burdening factors—population and per capita activity—parallel the increase and decrease of production levels. For the third factor (the nature of our activities), it roughly holds that the more burdensome for the environment our activities are, the higher their contribution is to national income, and vice versa. Thus, driving a car contributes more to GNP than riding a bicycle. This emerges from an analysis of the Dutch national accounts. The sectorial composition of the Dutch accounts does not differ appreciably from that of the United Kingdom, nor probably from that of most other Northern countries. What follows is therefore by and large valid for industrialized countries.

Production growth results largely from increase in productivity, in which the loss of scarce environmental goods has not been taken into account. Increase in labor volume plays a minor role. One-quarter to one-third of the activities making up national income (notably state consumption) do not contribute to its growth, because increase in productivity is difficult to measure. Other activities result only in slight improvements in productivity. Average annual growth must therefore be achieved by much higher growth among the remaining activities. Thirty percent of activities generate about 70 percent of growth. Unfortunately, these are precisely the activities that, by their use of space, soil, and resources, or by their pollution in production or consumption, harm the environment most. These are notably the oil, petrochemical, and metal industries, as well as agriculture, public utilities, road building, transport, and mining.

Measures to save the environment will have the following effects on growth rates and on production levels. To maintain current lifestyles as much as possible, all available technical measures should be applied to the fullest extent affordable. Such measures include end-of-pipe treatment, process-integrated changes, recycling, increasing energy efficiency, terracing agricultural slopes, and sustainably managing forests. Because they require extra labor input, these measures reduce labor productivity and therefore raise product prices, which in turn checks growth of national income (corrected for double counting). (The check of growth can be alleviated by the absorption of unemployed workers, up to the point where full employment has been attained.)

Saving the environment without causing a rise in prices and subsequent check of production growth is only possible if a technology is invented that is sufficiently clean, reduces the use of space sufficiently, leaves the soil intact, does not deplete energy and resources (that is, energy derived from the sun and recycling), *and* is cheaper (or at least not more expensive) than current technology. This is hardly imaginable for our whole range of current activities. But when such technologies become available, the above-mentioned effects will be avoided.

Applying technical measures cannot completely avoid a change in our consumption pattern, because price rises resulting from the measures inevitably cause a shift toward more environmentally benign activities, such as bicycling and using public transport.

Technical measures often do not really solve the problem, either because the growth of the activity overrides the effect of the measure, or because of the persistent and cumulative character of the burden. In this case, the measure only retards the rate of deterioration. Thus, to stop the Netherlands' contribution to acidification of forests and lakes, apart from applying all available technical means, the Dutch must reduce the number of car miles and farm livestock by about 50 percent (Fransen 1987). For some problems no technical measures are available: for instance, the loss of habitat of plant and animal species as a result of the use of space and the formation of cirrus clouds that contribute to the greenhouse effect. (CO_2 accumulation may be partly solvable.) In these cases, in addition to technical measures, a direct shift in behavior patterns must ensue, forced by do's and don'ts, rules, incentives, and taxes.

A direct shift in production and consumption patterns will also check GNP growth, as follows from the analysis of national accounts (the environmentally most burdensome activities contribute most to GNP growth). Moreover, in terms of national accounts, environmentally benign activities represent a smaller volume. Thus, a bicycle mile represents a smaller volume than a car mile; a sweater a smaller volume that a hot room; an extra blanket a smaller volume than heating the whole house; beans a smaller volume than meat; and a holiday by train a smaller volume than a holiday by plane. This is mainly because the exhaustion of environment and resources is not charged to national income as costs. If it were, the differences would become much smaller or nil.

From the above, it follows that saving the environment will certainly check production growth and probably lead to lower levels of national income. This outcome can hardly surprise. Many have known for a long time that population growth and rising production and consumption levels cannot be sustained forever in a finite world. The outcome of the above analysis should arouse optimism rather than pessimism, because environmentally benign activities are remarkably cheap. Thus, a bicycle is much cheaper than a car, a blanket is cheaper than central heating, and rearing two children is cheaper than bringing up ten. This means that saving our planet is indeed possible. Our fervent goal—to arrive at environmental sustainability, as advocated by the Brundtland Report (World Commission on Environment and Development 1987) and by politicians and institutions across the world—can indeed be fulfilled, albeit only under limiting conditions. In particular, population growth should be halted as soon as possible. Moreover, activities with little or no material throughput can increase practically forever. As we have seen, this will not result in a great increase in national income. Decision-makers should not become upset by this. Changes in national income levels by no means indicate the economic success of their policies, because they conceal the destruction of our life-support systems as long as the figures are not corrected for environmental losses.

Correction of National Income Based on Sustainable Use of the Environment

Attempts to correct national income for environmental losses started in the early 1970s with the following train of thought (Hueting 1980). The environment is interpreted as the physical surroundings of humanity, on which it is completely dependent (from breathing to producing). Within the environment, a number of possible uses can be distinguished. These are called environmental functions. When the use of a function by an activity is at the expense of the use of another (or the same) function by another activity, or threatens to be so in the future, loss of function occurs. Environmental functions then have become scarce goods, because the use of a function implies, wholly or partly, the sacrifice of another. This fully meets the definition of scarcity that demarcates the economic discipline. This approach links ecology and economics and places environment centrally in economic theory.

Because national income is recorded in market prices, shadow prices have to be estimated for functions (and their losses) that are directly comparable with prices of manmade marketed goods. For this purpose, supply and demand curves for functions have to be constructed. It appeared possible to construct supply curves, consisting of the costs of measures eliminating the burden on the environment, arranged by increasing costs per unit burden avoided. But in most cases no complete demand curves can be found. This is because the possibilities for preferences for environmental functions to be manifested via market behavior are very limited. Other methods, such as the willingness to pay or to accept, do not yield complete demand curves, certainly for functions on which current and future life depends. Standards setting was also considered, but the questions "What standards are to be set and by whom?" could not be answered at that time.

This situation has now changed. Especially after the 1987 Brundtland Report, politicians and organizations across the world declared themselves in favor of sustainable use of the environment. This preference, voiced by society, opens up the possibility of basing a calculation on standards for the sustainable use of environmental functions, instead of on (unknown) individual preferences.

Therefore, the following procedure is proposed for correcting GNP for environmental losses (Hueting 1986, 1989). First, define physical standards for environmental functions, based on their sustainable use. These standards replace the (unknown) demand curves. Then formulate measures to meet these standards. Finally, estimate the money involved in implementing the measures. The reduction of national income (Y) by the amounts found gives a first approximation of the activity level that, in line with the standards applied, is sustainable. Needless to say, a correction for double counting, mentioned earlier in this chapter, must also be made. If the sustainable level is Y', the difference between Y and Y' indicates, in monetary terms, how far society has drifted from its desired goal of sustainable use of the environment.

The standards can be related to environmental functions. Thus it is possible to formulate the way in which a forest should be managed in order to attain a sustainable use of its functions. Sustainability then means that all present and future uses remain available. For renewable resources such as forests, water, soil, and air, as long as their regenerative capacity remains intact, then the functions remain intact (for example, the function "supplier of wood" of forests, the function "drinking water" of water, the function "soil for raising crops" of soil, and the function "air for physiological functioning" of air). This means that emissions of substances that accumulate in the environment, such as PCBs, heavy metals, nitrates, and carbon dioxide, may not exceed the natural assimilative capacity of the environment, and that erosion rates may not exceed natural soil regeneration. As for nonrenewable resources, such as oil and copper, "regeneration" takes the form of research and bringing into practice flow resources such as energy derived from the sun (wind, tidal, collectors, photovoltaic cells), recycling of materials, and developing their substitutes.

The measures to meet standards include reforestation, building terraces, draining roads, maintaining landscape buffers, selective use of pesticides and fertilizers, building treatment plants, material recycling,

introducing flow energy, altering industrial processes, using more public transport and bicycles, and use of space that leaves sufficient room
for the survival of plant and animal species.

The method is applicable for cost-benefit analyses of projects with
long-term environmental effects. The method seems to be the only way
to confront national income with the losses of environmental functions in monetary terms. The physical data required for comparison
with standards come down to basic environmental statistics that have
to be collected in any case if a government is to get a grip on the state
of the environment. The formulation of measures to meet standards
and estimates of the expenditures involved are indispensable for policy
decisions.

In other words, the work for correcting national income figures
might be laborious, but it has to be done in any case if one wants to
practice a deliberate policy with respect to the environment. We therefore strongly urge decision-makers to stimulate this kind of research in
their countries. The Philippines and Sweden already are interested in
following the Dutch lead.

Our Debt to Future Generations

A rough order of magnitude of the debt to future generations the world
has been accumulating during the last few decades, and how it is to be
paid off, is estimated below. We base this on the use of energy and corresponding CO_2 emissions.

One aspect of sustainability could be that the annual consumption
of fuels such as coal, oil, and natural gas, expressed as a percentage of
known reserves, is equal to the rate of efficiency growth in the use of
energy, while keeping the level of production constant (Tinbergen
1990). Tinbergen (1990) found that a figure for this efficiency growth
close to reality is 1.67 percent. By this behavior, it would be theoreti-
cally possible to use a finite stock for an infinite period of time. However, it is not certain whether this would be feasible, because it would
mean that the production and consumption of today's package of goods
has to be generated with an ever-smaller amount of energy. Thus, after

315 years, today's package must be generated with 0.5 percent of to-day's energy use. This 315 years is a short period in relation to the speed of natural processes in question when addressing environmental sus-tainability. Therefore, if we also want to avoid the hazards of nuclear energy, development of new technologies such as flow energy (derived from the sun) is less risky.

To avoid greenhouse risks, global CO_2 emissions are estimated to have to be reduced by 75 to 80 percent. In the period 1950 to 1988, CO_2 emissions, energy use, and gross domestic product (GDP) ran parallel. Around 1950, both world GDP and energy use amounted to 25 percent of the 1988 level. This means that, other things being equal, the GDP level must be reduced by 75 percent. Assuming that a CO_2 reduction of 25 percent is possible at low cost, and considering that a number of environmental effects are not eliminated by reduced energy use, we conclude that to pay off global environmental debt we would have to halve the level of global activities. This demonstrates the urgency of allocating all available resources, such as know-how and capital, to-ward the development of new technologies (such as flow energy and recycling), instead of toward increasing production, while halting and then reversing population growth. The last thing the world can afford is to wage war, such as occurred in the Persian Gulf in 1991.

The outlook for such changes in technology seems to be promising. For example, Potma (1990) shows that techniques such as splitting water molecules by solar energy in deserts and transporting the result-ing hydrogen fuels can provide the world with sufficient clean energy at twice current energy prices. Desertic developing countries thus have a major export potential. This would allow a sustainable use of the en-vironment while regaining current production levels in fifty to a hun-dred years.

This is because sufficient clean energy would become available for both eliminating part of environmental effects other than the green-house effect and compensating for the necessary decrease in production where no solutions are available with additional production of another kind. Moreover, room would be created for raising per capita produc-tion levels in the South by a factor of 2.5. This would reduce the income gap between rich and poor countries from 10:1 to 4:1, with the condition of no further throughput growth in rich countries.

The uncertainties are, of course, far too big to attach great value to the outcome of this scenario. But the above clearly demonstrates that continuing prevailing growth paths is blocking our chances of survival, for which possibilities still remain.

Conclusion

In order to achieve sustainable use of the environment, we conclude that the highest priority should be accorded to devising and implementing economic policies that (1) accelerate development of new technologies, such as flow energy and recycling; (2) permit no further production growth in rich countries; (3) stabilize the global population as soon as possible; and (4) improve international income distribution.

References

Fransen, J. T. P. *Zure Regen: Een Nieuw Beleid.* Utrecht: Natuur en Milieu Foundation, 1987.

Hueting, R. *New Scarcity and Economic Growth.* Oxford: Oxford University Press, 1980.

Hueting, R. "A Note on the Construction of an Environmental Indicator in Monetary Terms as a Supplement to National Income with the Aid of Basic Environmental Statistics." Jakarta: Ministry of Population and Environment, 1986. [Available from the author.]

Hueting, R. "Correcting National Income for Environmental Losses: Towards a Practical Solution." In *Environmental Accounting for Sustainable Development,* edited by Y. Ahmad, S. El Serafy, and E. Lutz. Washington, D.C.: World Bank, 1989.

Potma, T. G. "Interrelationships Between Environment, Energy and Economy" (paper for the Dutch National Energy Authority). Delft: Center for Energy Conservation and Clean Technology, 1990.

Tinbergen, J. "How to Leave Enough Natural Resources for Future Generations?" *NRC Handelsblad,* 22 June 1990, p. 8 (in Dutch).

Tinbergen, J. "Le incognite del terzo millenio," *Dimensione Energia* 38 (Jan–Feb 1990): 36–41.

Tinbergen, J. Personal communication, 1991, and quoted in Hueting, 1980, pp. 153 and 157.

World Commission on Environment and Development. "Our Common Future" (The Brundtland Report). Oxford: Oxford University Press, 1987.

5

Sustainability, Income Measurement, and Growth

Salah El Serafy

Sustainability

Sustainability is a concept that has figured prominently in the Brundt-land Report, though it has proved difficult to define without ambiguity. Within the Brundtland Report itself we find more than one definition, but the one that has since been most quoted is the following: "Sustainable development is development that meets the needs of the present without compromising the ability of future generations to meet their own needs." The Report goes on to clarify sustainable development:

> It contains within it two key concepts:
>
> - the concept of "needs," in particular the essential needs of the world's poor, to which overriding priority should be given; and
>
> - the idea of limitations imposed by the state of technology and social organization on the environment's ability to meet present and future needs.[1]

The reference to limitations of technology and social organization and to meeting "essential needs of the world's poor" in the above quotation, and a later statement that "concern for social equity between generations . . . must logically be extended to equity within each generation," while appealing to many readers, emphasizes the complexity of Brundtland's sustainability, both as a concept and as a pragmatic guide to policy action. As discussed later in this chapter, the vagueness

63

of definition of Brundtland's sustainability should not detract from its valid concern for addressing distributional issues, which are viewed rightly as an integral part of the environmental problem. This ambiguity is by no means confined to Brundtland. A more recent attempt to clarify what sustainability meant to different authors yielded a bewildering array of definitions.[2]

The search for a precise meaning of sustainability has remained elusive, with a growing awareness now that for practical purposes sustainability should be perceived in approximate terms only.[3] It is certainly evident that the use of the expression "sustainable growth" has become more frequent in recent development literature, replacing the older unqualified "growth," in an apparent attempt to impart the notion that growth should be kept within environmental limits. The Brundtland Report represents one of the early attempts at this usage. It is true, however, that such environmental limits remain undefined in a manner conducive to practicable policy guidelines, but I return to this point later.

Brundtland's Impact

In retrospect it seems that while the Brundtland Report made a great impact on world leaders and environmentalists alike, its impact on economists has been rather modest. This is not to deny, however, some influence it has had on economic policy, indirectly through the political forces it has motivated.[4] The attention that has been given to global environmental issues since the publication of "Our Common Future" may be a product of its political impact.[5] There is also the growing coverage of environmental issues in economic work practically everywhere, which may be traced back, at least in part, to Brundtland's publication.

Environmental Accounting for Sustainable Development

While Brundtland was in gestation, an initiative was developing, spurred by the United Nations Environment Program (UNEP) and the

World Bank, to revise national income calculations in order to reflect in them environmental concerns. The coincidence in timing is remarkable between the World Commission on Environment and Development, which began its work in December 1983 and reached its conclusions in mid-1987, and the UNEP–World Bank workshops, which sought improved national income measurements. This parallel effort also began in 1983, reached a crucial stage in 1988, and is still progressing in a number of directions.[6]

During the past two decades most countries have been calculating their national income according to guidelines, issued in 1968 by the United Nations Statistical Office, generally known as the System of National Accounts (SNA). These guidelines paid practically no attention to the fact that, in order to reckon income properly, the SNA must account for natural resource erosion and environmental degradation. The old system treated much of the antipollution expenditures as final expenditures that would raise income, instead of regarding them as necessary intermediate costs that should be charged against the final products. It also failed to take account of environmental disasters when they occurred. It treated natural resources, particularly those emanating from the public sector, as a free gift from nature, reflecting in the accounts mainly their direct extraction costs and any valuation, over and above extraction cost, that the uneven and heterogeneous free market deigned to attach to them.

Worst of all, the SNA failed to distinguish between value added by factors of production and sale of natural assets such as forestry products and petroleum. Through income measurements patterned on the SNA, many natural-resource-based developing countries were made out to have higher income than they actually had and to be growing at rates that obscured their true economic performance. Besides, the accounts failed to reflect the fact that the current levels of prosperity they were enjoying would not last, since the basis for such prosperity was progressively being eroded. False accounting resulted from mixing in the flow accounts elements of natural capital that should have been kept separate from current income. Such income measurements, where they occurred, covered up economic weaknesses that needed urgent attention, thus misdirecting economic policy. Countries where natural resources contributed significantly to fiscal and external balance failed to make essential adjustments and ended up allocating to consumption too much of the receipts they obtained from selling their natural assets. Many of them assumed too much external debt for their own good. Domestically, relative prices moved against tradeable goods, resulting in a lamentable shrinkage of non-natural, resource-based activities. Little wonder that so many resource-rich developing countries that should have benefited from the exceptional improvement of their terms of trade in the 1970s found themselves in the 1980s hardly better off than they had been before.[7]

At the UNEP–World Bank workshop held in Paris in November 1988, experts from various national statistical offices met with economists and others who had been investigating the topic of environmental national accounting, and for the first time a consensus was reached that natural resources and the environment were indeed important and likely to become more so in the future; that natural accounts should reflect the stress on the environment that had become increasingly evident; and that a set of environmental satellite accounts needed to be elaborated and attached to the new SNA core accounts, with the view of reflecting environmental considerations. That 1988 meeting was a watershed from which significant developments were to flow. Further work since then, conducted in cooperation with the United Nations Statistical Office, has led to the acceptance of the notion that when the revised SNA (expected in 1993) came out, it would recommend compiling a set of satellite environmental accounts showing to the extent possible the changes that occur from year to year in the state of the environment and attempting a recalculation of national income to reflect such changes. This national accounting adjustment initiative, which still continues, has provided a bridge between some of the objectives of the environmentalists and the work of the economists.

Sustainability and Income

If properly measured, income is sustainable by definition. From an environmental angle, errors in measuring income can be viewed as coming largely from wrongly mixing in income certain elements of natural capital, and from confusion of inventory liquidation with depreciation of fixed assets.[8] A person or a nation cannot continue to live at the same material level if present enjoyment is obtained at the cost of liquidating capital. As capital is eroded, the ability to maintain the same level of consumption into the future is undermined. That is why, from its inception, the accounting profession has insisted that for profit and loss calculations, whether for individuals or corporations, capital must be "kept intact." To the accountant, keeping capital intact never meant that capital should be preserved in its original state (the preservationist argument), but only that allowance be made out of current income in order to restore capital to the extent that it has eroded. Unless capital is "maintained," future income would inevitably decline. By extension of the same argument to the area of national accounting, keeping capital, including environmental capital, intact for accounting purposes requires adjusting income to reflect capital deterioration. Again, this does not mean that the accountant is advocating that capital should be kept undisturbed, or in the language of some environmentalists, that it should be "preserved" in its existing state, since the very essence of sustaining economic activity relies on utilizing capital to generate future profits or income. There is little disagreement now on extending the same principles that apply to manmade capital to environmental capital, save on the application of those principles to the special case of depletable resources, which cannot be renewed or recycled, but whose stock steadily dwindles as it is used up in the productive process.

That the environment can be viewed as natural capital is easy to perceive, both as a sink for wastes and a source of materials and energy.[9] Wastes have been dumped in rivers and seas, buried on land, and dispersed in the atmosphere in the belief that such natural receptors had an unlimited capacity to receive them. As production has grown, this capacity has clearly been seen to be limited and has also become limiting. There is thus growing acceptance of the notion that the polluting activities should bear the full costs to society of their pollution. If standards are set for acceptable levels of pollution, the cost of achieving such standards, even if not actually incurred, can be used as a measure of environmental deterioration on account of pollution and be charged against income as depreciation.

As a source of materials, the environment should also be brought into income calculation. A distinction is clearly needed between resources that can be regenerated and others that cannot. Nature, and society in cooperation with nature, can amend, restore, or regenerate fish stocks, forests, soils, and the like. Where such regeneration falls short of theoretical or practical rates that would maintain such capital intact (that is, at its original level at the beginning of each accounting period), shortfalls should be deducted, as depreciation, from gross income calculations. Some problems of valuation would present themselves, but the guiding principle throughout should be pragmatism and approximation, since precise measurement is still, and likely to remain, an unattainable goal. Ecologists, likewise, should attempt measurements of sustainable yield in the same spirit of providing pragmatic and prudential estimates, instead of letting their quest for precision become an obstacle that would render their measurements irrelevant for policy.

With respect to depletable minerals such as fossil fuels, which cannot be meaningfully restored once they are used, applying the same approach of depreciation as in the case of renewable resources would be inappropriate. Such resources represent known wealth that can be liquidated over a variable time span depending on their owners' needs, their expectations of future prices, and the state of the market. While productive capacity is depreciated, existing inventories are used up or liquidated, and it would be wrong conceptually to include the proceeds from selling inventories in gross income. And it is equally wrong to believe that, in order to correct for their inclusion in gross income, all that is needed is to deduct the decline of the stock from the wrongly calculated gross income to arrive at a correctly measured net income. If such an approach is adopted, neither the gross nor the net income will be correctly measured. The gross will be inflated by asset sales that do not represent value added, and the net will be underestimated, since the whole contribution of the exploitation activity to income is removed as capital consumption or depreciation. If, on top of such erro-

neous accounting we add windfalls from upward reestimation of reserves, and deduct from income downward adjustments of these
reserves, we arrive at very dubious and gyrating estimates of income
that are as meaningless as they are useless, either for gauging economic
performance or for guiding economic policy. A depletable resource's
contribution to income requires special handling.

Accounting for Depletable Resources

In as much as the reserves of depletable resources are ascertained, they
should be treated as inventories, not as fixed capital. Inventories can be
drawn down to exhaustion if that is perceived by their owners as economically desirable. The proceeds from their exploitation in any one
accounting period should, as a first step, be viewed as proceeds from
asset sales, not as value added. If the owners draw down all their known
reserves in one year because they believe this to be best in light of their
assessment of future prices, it would obviously be wrong to include all
such proceeds in their gross income for that year and to deduct the diminution of the asset, equivalent to the same amount that had been included in gross income, so that net income from this activity is shown
as zero. Now that the owners have substituted for the subsoil asset, say,
a bank account, true income is the interest that can be earned on the
new account. Alternatively, the owners may sink the proceeds from
selling the mineral assets in new material investments whose *returns*
would represent true income. In this way capital liquidation would be
kept, as it should, outside the flow accounts.

Following a proposition by the late Professor Sir John Hicks, which
he put forward half a century ago,[10] it was possible for me to calculate
that part of the proceeds from a wasting asset that must be reinvested
in alternative assets so that the yields obtained from such reinvest-
ments would compensate for the decline in receipts from the wasting
asset. Using a discount rate and the amount extracted from the reserves
in any one year relative to total reserves, I was able to indicate the proportion of the proceeds that can be reckoned as true income, the re-
mainder—a kind of a Keynesian user cost—having to be set aside and

reinvested to produce an aggregate stream of constant future income. The user cost part is a capital element that should be expunged from the gross domestic product (GDP) or gross income and therefore would not appear in the net domestic product or net income either. If fresh deposits are located, these would affect the flow accounts only indirectly through the change of the reserves-to-extraction ratio—that is, providing a longer lifetime of the asset so that the income part rises and the user cost part falls.[11]

This proposal, which is slowly gaining ground among economists, is still by no means generally accepted, either by them or by the national income statisticians.[12] Many of the latter, even if convinced, would still prefer to preserve old-time series of erroneously calculated GDP along conventional lines on the argument that all that is required is to deduct natural resource "depreciation," equivalent to the entire diminution of stock, from the gross product to show a more sustainable net product that would amount to nil. The conceptual confusion implied by such procedures has already been mentioned. If one must persist with this confusion for the sake of preserving old-time series, the user cost, as explained above, would be the appropriate estimate of "depreciation."

The Limited Function of Accounting

Accounting, by its nature, has a limited function. It is essentially a backward-looking activity attempting to sort out from the behavior of economic units during a past period elements from which an arithmetical history is compiled. This usually takes the form of a snapshot at a point in time (a balance sheet of assets and liabilities) and a flow, during a certain period (most commonly a year), of net results of the economic activity concerned: profits and loss for an individual or a corporation and value added for a nation. Economists have often misunderstood the functions of the accountant, and his concern—perhaps obsession— with keeping capital intact, often challenging the accountant's meaning of keeping capital intact and the accuracy of his measurements, since such a concept of capital maintenance inevitably refers to the future. The Hicksian definition of income itself, whose author insisted that it was merely a rough guide for prudent behavior, has wrongly been criticized on the economist's usual ground of concern with precision and his (the economist's) forward—rather than the accountant's back-ward—orientation. Hicks's income has been said to be incapable of being "directly measured" and even that it is "not suited to an account-ing of what happened in the past" either.[13] Whereas Hicks stressed the accountant's quest for approximately defining a level of *income* that can be devoted to consumption with concern for a sustainability built around the reuse of capital in the future, other economists have tended to hanker after a precise level of sustainability that the Hicksian ap-proach, with its emphasis on *future* income sustainability, obviously cannot meet, partly because the future will always remain unknown.

Economists and accountants have different, but perfectly reconcil-able, objectives. In their measurements the accountants seek approxi-mations, assume constant technology, and posit that the future will be a continuation of the past. In practice, technology does change, and the future is a little different from the past. But this does not matter much, however, since the accountants' accounting period is seldom more than one year, and every new year brings with it new facts and some fresh technology that the accountants have to, and certainly do, take in their stride.

Businesses and Governments

The approach I have proposed for estimating income from depletable natural resources, which relies on setting aside part of the proceeds from the sale of natural capital to be sunk in alternative investments so that they may yield a constant stream of future income, begs the ques-tion as to what kind of alternative investments are available, and whether for the sake of sustainability such investments will always be available. Here we leave the ex post world of the accountant and enter the realm of ex ante analysis.

Individual owners of depletable resources usually see to it that part of their receipts, whether in the form of depletable allowances or set-asides, are reinvested so that the owners can continue in business. Whether or not their new investments should be in the same line of business they are already in, or diverted toward other lines, depends on many factors. If the price of the natural resource they own rises in reflection of its growing scarcity, thus indicating the opportunity for investment to produce substitutes based on renewable resources, and if such a course is economically feasible, the owners may well continue in the same line of business. But frequently the market would fail to reflect the resource's growing scarcity, and its price would fail to rise. Besides, technologies for producing substitutes may not be available, and if available may not be economic at the prevailing set of prices. Thus we often observe a tendency for diversification away from one-product business on the part of large corporations that exploit natural resources.

Some environmentalists would prefer that the user cost entailed in the exploitation of a depletable natural asset be invested in a "twin" project that would supply a renewable substitute for the same depletable source.[14] But in light of the considerations just mentioned, such "twinning" or "pairing" may not be attractive to private owners. On the other hand, there is nothing against society as a whole indicating its desire to raise the overall level of savings and investment so that these become consistent with the objective of future income sustainability and also subsidize pioneering and experimental ventures in pursuit of finding renewable sources to replace the diminishing ones. This can be done by insisting, through appropriate monetary and fiscal policies, that the user cost of depletable resource exploitation should be added to current investments. The extra investments would be guided to socially desirable ventures, such as natural resource restoration and maintenance, through a carefully designed system of taxation and subsidies.

User Cost and Income Identities

Consider what happens to the usual identity that income, Y, is the sum total of consumption, C, and investment, I. Denoting user cost by the letter U, we can write:

$$Y = C + I \tag{1}$$

Adjusting for user cost, equation (1) becomes:

$$Y - U = (C - U) + I \tag{2}$$

If the user cost is devoted to fresh investments, income rises and we get:

$$Y = (C - U) + (I + U) \tag{3}$$

Equation (3) is thus seen to be identical to equation (1) except that consumption is lower and investment is higher.

Equation (2), however, depicts the correct level of income if the user cost is not reinvested. But if C remains unchanged, then the true level of investment that has been attained is only $I - U$ since U represents a disinvestment. In this latter case we have:

$$Y - U = C + (I - U) \tag{4}$$

Policy and the Problem of Scale

While the approach of sinking part of the proceeds into new investments seems perfectly valid for individuals, businesses, and even small countries, which also have the option of acquiring foreign investments if profitable domestic opportunities are not available, is it workable if it is done on a large scale so that significant portions of global natural capital might be liquidated to be substituted for by manmade capital formation?

Once the problem is posed in this way, the realization of the objective of creating a permanent income stream from wasting assets becomes questionable. Individuals, corporations, and even nations can run out of a natural resource—even if their livelihoods depend materially on it—in the knowledge that future income may be generated through carefully selected new investments. When considering better accounting for depletable resources, my focus was on the *income* of their owners. It did not matter what form the new investments would take, provided they guaranteed for the owners a constant stream of future income. The form of the new investments would be guided by the market, and if the market indicated that the new investments should be in the same line of business, so be it. However, if the problem is considered not just as one of better accounting for the resource owners, but in a forward context as a guide to economic policy on a global scale, we have to face the issues raised by Brundtland and the various constraints and propositions we find there for future environmental directions. We also encounter the problems of scale and of ultimate substitutability between natural resources and manmade capital to which Herman Daly has been drawing our attention.

If we perceive the problem globally, then it is clearly necessary to replace, for example, dwindling natural energy sources, not just with other sources of *income*, but with other sources of *energy* that are renewable, and the issue of "twinning" becomes relevant. If the market fails to signal rising energy prices to justify investing in renewable energy sources, then society may wish to give the market a helping hand through appropriate policy. Viewed globally, society should have a broad interest in the creation and application of new technologies that would substitute renewable sources for diminishing, nonrenewable ones.

But what should be done about the search for an equilibrium between the state of the environment and global economic activity? The world economic organization has been functioning on the basis of economic agents seeking perpetual economic growth, a pursuit that has traditionally been seen not only as desirable for raising material welfare all around but also as essential for energizing the development of the less developed countries and thus assisting in the alleviation of poverty. If technology could be organized so that it gave us substitutes for natural resources through the instrument of manmade capital formation, we would be able to continue "business as usual," hoping that the market would reflect scarcities into higher prices and thus guide this process of substitution. This certainly appears to be one of Brundtland's fundamental assumptions. However, we have reached a stage where the state of the environment has become so stressed, and technology and social organization have clearly lagged, at least so far, that some drastic alternative solution deserves to be explored.

Brundtland offered one solution, which leans toward maintaining the current emphasis on growth while using the fruits of growth to lessen the material throughput in economic activity, to repair the environment, and also to redistribute income, both intranationally and from the richer to the poorer nations, with the objective of alleviating poverty. I join with the other contributors to this volume in contending that this strategy is questionable—partly because much of the damage to the environment caused by indiscriminate growth is irreversible; partly because the process of substitution of manmade capital for natural resources is slow and erratic; and also in view of the enormous increase projected for global economic activity as compared with the advanced state of environmental stress already reached. If we are serious about saving our planet, we must seek a steady state for the economies of the rich, while the poor grow and develop so that poverty is eradicated and income disparity, which is the source of so much environmental damage, is reduced. Meanwhile technology development and dissemination should be accelerated and population growth urgently halted.

If the Brundtland path is rejected as impractical, can the proposal to arrest growth in much of the world economy be viewed as anything short of utopian? It is difficult specifically to perceive the sociology and political economy of maintaining a steady level of income in the richer countries. Such countries rely primarily on free market forces to guide the allocation of economic resources. In these countries, the essential profit motive is geared unavoidably to business expansion in search of opportunity. The impact of the richer countries' economic expansion on developing countries has also often been seen as benign in an "empty world" context of nonbinding environmental constraints. In fact, every time growth slows down in the richer countries, the poorer ones appear to suffer from depressed incomes and adverse terms of trade. And yet the richer countries use the bulk of the world resources to support a minority of the world population. If the rich are to grow richer merely to provide markets for the poor, not only are there more economical ways to achieve the same objective, but such a course would accelerate international income inequality.

Clearly something drastic has to take place in social and industrial organization and in the modalities of international relations if a steady state of economic activity, involving a constant level of throughput, is to prevail in the developed countries. Drafting a blueprint for this vision of the future is essential. Its economic content will have to address the problem of obtaining growth and/or development in the poorer countries simultaneously as the economies of the richer countries are kept on an even keel. In addition, the richer countries would be asked to transfer to the less developed countries the resources necessary to redress the negative effect of the richer countries' arrested growth and to alleviate poverty. Furthermore, it is necessary to plan for the kind of economic policy that would have to apply in the richer countries to produce the target of a steady state: as some activities will have to expand, others must contract. What criteria would be used to modulate aggregate activity in a free market economy that also has to be managed in pursuit of many other policy objectives? The issues this scenario raises will have to be faced by the advocates of such a strategy.[15] The Brundtland Report avoided all these complex issues and opted instead for a nonrevolutionary, rather optimistic, but seemingly untenable course.

Conclusion

Finally, a word about the importance of proper income accounting, since it is income measurements that will indicate what kind of growth or expansion of economic activity is being experienced and projected. Today's income changes, which probably lie behind Brundtland's projections of growth, relate to the gross domestic product (GDP) as conventionally measured and as valued at factor cost.[16] But if we shift the focus from the gross product to an environmentally more sustainable *net* product (from which the user cost of depletable resources has been eliminated), put a value on natural disasters and deduct this from income, and develop the habit of valuing activities at their full environmental cost when prices reflect true scarcities, we are bound to get a very different reading of income and its growth. In which case it might well turn out that the five-to-ten-times expansion in economic activity, as envisaged by Brundtland and stressed by McNeill, will be less.[17] A hint of this is to be found in the contribution by Tinbergen and Hueting in this volume (see Chapter 4), but clearly much work is needed to clarify this issue.

Notes

1. World Commission on Environment and Development, "Our Common Future" (The Brundtland Report) (Oxford: Oxford University Press, 1987), 43.

2. Definitions of sustainability are surveyed by J. Pezzey in Appendix 1, "Definitions of Sustainability in the Literature," of *Economic Analysis of Sustainable Growth and Sustainable Development* (Environment Department Working Paper 15) (Washington, D.C.: World Bank, 1989).

3. As the reader will note, presently the search for a precise meaning of "sustainability" is akin to defining "income" in exact terms. No unanimity is possible, since both concepts depend upon one's vision of the future. For practical purposes, however, and as a guide for prudent behavior, we must be content with some useful degree of approximation.

4. Whether it was the Brundtland Report itself, or the political forces that have been gathering momentum independently in various parts of the richer nations, it is remarkable how the impact of the Green Movement has been reflected in the declarations of recent economic summits of the Group of Seven leading industrial nations and through the latter's influence has given vent to a number of environmental initiatives. The July 1989 Economic Declaration of the G-7 Economic Summit (section 37) contained the statements: "In order to achieve sustainable development, we shall ensure the compatibility of economic growth and development with the protection of the environment" and "We encourage the World Bank and regional development banks to integrate environmental considerations into their activities."

5. The July 1990 Economic Declaration of the G-7 Economic Summit referred to global environmental stress (ozone depletion, climate change, marine pollution, and loss of biological diversity) and stated that "one of our most important responsibilities is to pass on to future generations an environment whose health, beauty and economic potential are not threatened."

6. It is interesting that in their initial stages the UNEP–World Bank work shops, after establishing national physical indicators of environmental stress,

were seeking to combine these eventually into one national index that would reflect the state of the environment, but participants very quickly realized that a system of "weighting" (or valuation) was necessary to produce such a single index. This moved the concern of the workshops quite early in the direction of reforming national income measurement. Cf. S. El Serafy's "Rapporteur's Report of the October 1985 Paris Meeting" (Washington, D.C.: World Bank, 1986), mimeographed.

7. Cf. Alan Gelb and Associates, *Oil Windfalls: Blessing or Curse?* (World Bank Research Publication) (Oxford: Oxford University Press, 1988).

8. I am abstracting here from a number of activities that have traditionally been excluded from national income reckoning, such as household services by family members. That the environment can be viewed as capital, contributing to the productive process, is a notion that is entirely in harmony with neoclassical economic thinking. See Salah El Serafy, "The Environment as Capital," *Ecological Economics: The Science and Management of Sustainability*, ed. R. Costanza (New York: Columbia University Press, 1991).

9. See El Serafy, "The Environment as Capital," in *Ecological Economics*, op. cit.

10. J. R. Hicks, *Value and Capital*, 2d ed. (Oxford: Clarendon Press, 1946), 187.

11. Hicks's all too brief coverage of this topic in *Value and Capital* shows that he regarded such a user cost as an allowance for depreciation. In a personal communication in 1987, however, he indicated approval of my line of thinking and that I had "made good use of the income chapter in *Value and Capital*."

12. A qualified acceptance of this approach is to be found in M. A. Adelman, Harindar De Silva, and Michael F. Koehn, *User Cost in Oil Production* (Cambridge, Mass.: MIT Center for Energy Policy Research, October 1990). This work uses the calculations of El Serafy to adjust national income for a number of countries in support of arguments made in the text, but states that "El Serafy . . . err[s] in supposing that production can proceed at a constant rate, then abruptly cease. The decline rate stands at the center of every reservoir engineering calculation. Moreover the rate of extraction is limited by sharply rising marginal costs . . . However, this correction would not basically change the problem." It should be mentioned, however, that Adelman belongs to the camp that sees no scarcity developing in the supply of minerals, which he views correctly as inventories, but believes that "only a fraction of the minerals in the earth's crust, or in any given field, will ever be used (op. cit., p. 1). The approach I have been advocating is one that relies on a standard accountant's rule of thumb that

estimates inventory use out of a given stock in an attempt to approximate reality. I stated in my 1981 *Journal of Energy and Development* article that factors such as the ones mentioned by Adelman et al. could be accommodated under the approach I proposed. The so-called reservoir engineering rule of always keeping a constant ratio between reserves and extraction is of dubious reliability and not essential for the calculations in any case. See Salah El Serafy, "Absorptive Capacity, the Demand for Revenue and the Supply of Petroleum," *Journal of Energy and Development* 7 (Autumn 1981): 73–88.

13. See David F. Bradford, "Comment on Scott and Eisner," *Journal of Economic Literature* 28 (September 1990): 1184. This was a comment on Maurice Scott's "Extended Accounts for National Income and Product: A Comment" and Robert Eisner's "Reply" to Scott in the same issue.

14. Ecologists tend to define substitutes more narrowly than economists, who appear to favor a broad definition that allows the market freedom to define what a substitute is. David Pearce, Anil Markandya, and Edward Barbier, in their *Blueprint for a Green Economy* (London: Earthscan Publications, 1989), advocated "pairing" or "twinning," but within a program of many projects rather than for each project at a time.

15. A vision of a possible course is offered in Herman E. Daly and John B. Cobb, *For the Common Good* (Boston: Beacon Press, 1989). Many aspects of such a course, however, need to be much more carefully examined, as the authors urge.

16. The convention of valuing GDP at factor costs and not at market prices derives from the presumption that taxes and subsidies represent deviations from genuine values produced by the market and that they should provide weights for the various activities that make up the domestic product. But if a new set of environmentally inspired taxes and subsidies is viewed as necessary to correct the market's failure to put proper values on the services of natural resources, then we should regard the new, environmentally adjusted "market prices" as better weights than factor costs for the purpose of estimating income in the present context.

17. James McNeill, "Sustainable Development, Economics and the Growth Imperative" (paper presented to the Workshop on the Economics of Sustainable Development) (Washington, D.C.: U.S. Environmental Protection Agency, January 1990).

6

Project Evaluation
and Sustainable Development

Raymond Mikesell

Some development economists and most environmentalists advocate the adoption of sustainable development in place of economic growth as the primary objective for both industrial and developing countries. Sustainable development has also been endorsed by the World Bank and other multilateral development banks (MDBs) and by bilateral assistance agencies such as the United States Agency for International Development. An essential ingredient in sustainable development is the conservation of the natural resource base for use by future generations. However, there are a number of difficulties in specifying and applying sustainability as a criterion for evaluating individual projects.

The purpose of this chapter is to present a method of project evaluation that is consistent with the principles of sustainable development. The projects with which this chapter is concerned are those that require significant amounts of natural resources in their production or have a significant impact on natural resources in their construction or operation. Most of the projects supported by the multilateral development banks are resource-intensive, and many of them have adverse environmental impacts.

The traditional method of determining the financial feasibility of projects used by the World Bank and other development assistance agencies has been to calculate the internal rate of return on invested capital. If the internal rate of return exceeds a specified level (usually equal to the international long-term rate of interest plus an allowance for risk), the project is acceptable.[1] This approach to project evaluation implies that we should maximize the productivity of capital as the limiting factor. Sustainable development, on the other hand, implies that natural resources rather than capital are the scarcest, or limiting, factors in production (see Chapter 2). Hence, governments and MDBs should favor those projects that maximize the productivity of the natural resources used in the project. This requires that project proponents evaluate projects by calculating their net present value, assuming infinitely elastic supplies of labor and capital in combination with a fixed amount of natural resources. This approach has long been used in resource economics for evaluating resource projects.

Another characteristic of sustainable development is its concern with social benefits and costs, and not simply with the net returns to the owners of the factors of production. Sustainable development requires that we evaluate projects by calculating their net present social value (NPSV) rather than their net present value to private owners of the projects. Social benefits and costs include a host of externalities that may benefit or harm society.

Moreover, social costs involve the nonmonetary impacts of projects, such as illness and loss of environmental amenities, the monetary values of which require special methodologies to estimate. To an increasing degree, the World Bank and other development assistance agencies are concerned with social benefits and costs when evaluating projects, but they rarely include nonmonetary social costs in calculating financial feasibility.

The most distinguishing characteristic of sustainable development is the goal of intergenerational equity—that the present generation does not impair the resource base required by future generations to maintain or increase their well-being. This goal is variously defined, but the most widely accepted definition is a condition of nondecreasing per capita well-being across generations.[2] However, the conditions for achieving this goal involve the rate of population growth, technological developments for substituting more abundant for scarce resources, income distribution, and government policies that induce conservation of natural resources. All of these factors cannot be taken into account in evaluating individual projects. Hence, it is necessary to formulate some simple rules that would make individual projects compatible with the goal of sustainable development.

Sustainability requires that productivity of the resource base be maintained over time, either by renewing the resource or by investing in other capital assets an amount equal to the capital value of the resource depletion. Failure to deduct resource depletion overstates the net revenue of projects and consequently overstates their rate of return, leading to misallocation—that is, overinvestment in nonrenewable types of exploitation relative to other investments. I would satisfy the sustainability criterion in project evaluation by including in social costs any reduction in the value of the resource base caused by the construction and operation of the project. The resource base includes all natural and environmental resources that contribute to the production of both marketable and nonmarketable goods and services that provide utilities for human beings. Thus a project that significantly reduces the productivity of the land or the quality of the atmosphere, or of rivers and lakes, or of biodiversity, gives rise to social costs. This implies that the social costs are potentially measurable.

Treating Resource Depletion as a Social Cost

In the approach I here advocate, project evaluation is based on the NPSV of a project involving the use of natural resources, with any resource depletion arising directly or indirectly from the project treated as a social cost. The value of a resource depletion is the capitalized (discounted) value of the stream of utilities that could have been produced by using the lost resource in either the same type of project or in an alternative use of the resource, such as preserving an old-growth forest as an alternative to harvesting the timber. It is this capitalized value that we want to preserve for future generations; hence, the capitalized value of the resource loss must be preserved by an equivalent alternative investment that will benefit future generations.

In treating natural resource depletion as a social cost in project evaluation, a twofold problem arises. How do you measure the value of the depletion, and how much do you need to save and reinvest out of proj-

ect revenue to maintain the same income (after allowance for depletion) for future generations? The revenue from a resource project that is
attributed to the natural resource is the total receipts from the sale of
the products less the capital and labor costs associated with the project.
We may divide this revenue, R, into two components: the income component, X, and a capital component, $R - X$, representing the natural resource depletion (as proposed by El Serafy).[3] We need to define $R - X$ in
a way that it can be used as a social cost in the calculation of NPSV.
Assume we have a mine with annual receipts, R, that fully depletes in
n years, and that each year a portion of the revenue, $R - X$, is saved and
invested to allow for depletion, leaving X as income for the mine owners. For sustainability of the resource, $R - X$ should be sufficient to accumulate a fund by the termination of the mine that would enable the
owners to receive an infinite series of X, assuming a rate of interest of
r. Since the mine depletes in n years, the annual value of the depletion
is R, but if R is saved each year, X would be zero and none of the revenue
would be available for consumption.

The amount needed to be saved each year, $R - X$, is the present value
of the annual resource depletion, which we may express as $\dfrac{R}{(1+r)^n}$, so
that $X = R - \dfrac{R}{(1+r)^n}$. The proof is as follows: Using the standard formula for compounding 1 per annum at r:

$$\left(\frac{R}{(1+r)^n}\right)\left(\frac{(1+r)^{n-1}}{r}\right) = \frac{R - \dfrac{R}{(1+r)^n}}{r} = \frac{X}{r}$$

If $\dfrac{R}{(1+r)^n}$ is saved and compounded each year for n years at an interest
rate of r, the accumulated amount will equal $\dfrac{X}{r}$, which will provide a
perpetual income of X. Alternatively, the present value of R per year for
n years also equals $\dfrac{X}{r}$.[4]

The above analysis can be made clear with a numerical example. Assume R is \$250,000 per year and that the life of the mine is twenty years
and the rate of interest 10 percent. Using the above formula, the present

value of R per year for twenty years is \$2,130,000, and annual income, X, is \$213,000. Annual depletion, or $R - X$, equals \$37,000, which when saved and compounded at 10 percent over twenty years also equals \$2,130,000. The longer the life of the mine and the higher the rate of interest, the smaller the proportion of R that needs to be saved for depletion. For a mine that depletes in ten years, and assuming an interest rate of 5 percent, 75 percent of R would need to be saved for depletion. This compares with 15 percent in the first example.

Calculating the NPSV

The NPSV of the mine is the present value of an annual stream, $R - \left(\dfrac{R}{(1+r)^n}\right)$, or R minus the present value of annual depletion. This annual stream is also X per year, and the present value of X per year for n years is $\dfrac{X\left(1 - \dfrac{1}{(1+r)^n}\right)}{r}$, which equals the NPSV of the mine.

In the numerical example given above, the NPSV for a mine with a life of twenty years and a rate of interest of 10 percent is about \$1.8 million. With a higher annual depletion, the NPSV is much smaller. Thus, for a mine with a life of only ten years, depletion is 35 percent of R, and X is 65 percent of R—as against 15 percent of R for depletion and 85 percent for X, or income, in the example given above.

We may generalize the example given above by stating that the NPSV of a project with allowance for resource depletion is the present value of an annual stream $R - \dfrac{RD}{(1+r)^n}$, where RD is the average annual resource depletion during the life of the project. The actual resource depletion might take place at any time rather than in equal amounts over the life of the project. However, in order to satisfy the sustainability criterion, it makes little difference to future generations when the actual depletion takes place during the life of the project, say, twenty-five years. Resource depletion need not be confined to the depletion of reserves in a mining project. It may take the form of environmental damage caused by a mine or any other project that reduces the productivity of natural resources. For example, a mining operation might pollute a river, thereby reducing the value of the fish catch. The present value of the loss of fish catch would be a part of the social cost of the mine, thereby lowering the NPSV of the mining project. Alternatively, a hydroelectric dam might cause environmental damage to the recreational values of a river. If the damage is very large, $R - \dfrac{RD}{(1+r)^n}$ might be negative, as would also the NPSV of the project.

In calculating the NPSV, there should be an allowance for risk by applying probability coefficients to each of the relevant variables to estimate the expected NPSV of the project.

Reinvesting the Resource Depletion

In the approach to project evaluation outlined above, it makes no difference whether the accumulated depreciation is reinvested in renewing the depleted resource or used for some other capital improvement, so long as the investment yields a net social output equal to that lost by the depletion of the resource. The paradigm is the reinvestment of depreciation of a building or a machine. If a project destroys an old-growth forest or part of a scenic river, the reduced value of the resource as a producer of utilities should be compensated by an investment that will yield a stream of utilities equal to that which was lost. The investment may take the form of restoring the depleted natural resource, creating manmade physical capital, or improving human knowledge and skills for increasing the productivity of the resource base.

Three problems arise in rendering the above model consistent with sustainability. First, changing the system of accounting to include resource depletion as a social cost will not necessarily induce private entities to save and reinvest social capital. Private firms and individuals may still treat natural resource depletion as income available for consumption, and, except for depletion allowances for some types of natural resource exploitation, the tax system will count resource depletion as taxable income. Therefore, sustainability would require resource depletion to be taxed by the state and reinvested in a manner that will sustain output for future generations. The tax will, of course, be passed on to consumers. The prices for products whose production involves heavy resource depletion would be relatively higher than prices of products that contribute less to depletion. The state could either invest the revenues directly, or use the revenues to induce private investment for increasing the social product.

The second problem is what social investments made or induced by the state will ensure that future generations receive the capitalized value of the resources depleted by the present generation. Suppose that most of the tax revenue is invested in roads and buildings, rather than in restoring depleted renewable natural resources or in increasing the productivity of natural resources. How far can we go in substituting manmade physical capital for natural resource capital and still maintain a rising national or world output? I do not think we can assume that the aggregate national or world production function is a Cobb-Douglas production function in which the productive factors are completely substitutable.

Herman Daly argues in Chapter 2 that substitution of manmade capital for natural resources is quite limited. In other words, unless the raw material base is maintained, long-run sustainability is impossible. This position is highly controversial, and some resource economists believe that we can offset considerable resource depletion by increasing the productivity of natural resource capital. Without further discussion of this issue, I believe that sustainability requires that a substantial amount of the resource depletion be invested in replenishing renewable resources, in increasing product output per unit of resource input, or in increasing the end-use efficiency of resource-intensive products.

A third problem concerns substitutability on the demand side. How far can we go in satisfying the demand for wilderness amenities, clean air, and living space with manmade goods? There is surely a point beyond which further degradation of the environment cannot be compensated by higher per capita real incomes in the form of produced goods and services. What is the utility trade-off in driving a Cadillac or Mercedes in a perpetual traffic jam surrounded by foul air against walking through a grove of ancient redwoods? There are also limits on the extent to which we can allow the natural environment to deteriorate and still survive as a species.

Technological progress can offset depletion of the resource base by increasing the productivity of the remaining resources. It can also facilitate the substitution of manmade capital assets for natural resources and the substitution of more abundant for scarce natural resources in production. However, technological progress is necessary to maintain or increase per capita utilities of future generations with a rising population. I have not included technological progress in the calculation of the social costs represented by the depletion of the resource base for two reasons.

First, we do not know enough about future technology to assess its impact on the productivity of the resources used in particular projects. Second, we should allow technological progress to have its full effect on improving the well-being of future generations—that is, we should not borrow against future uncertain technological progress to finance present consumption in excess of what is sustainable with present technology. Thus, I believe the social costs of the depletion of the natural resources attributable to a project should be based on the current state of technology.

Criteria for MDB Support of Projects

For a project to qualify for MDB support, the expected NPSV adjusted for resource depletion should be positive. The expected NPSV of a proposed project, without allowance for resource depletion, is frequently regarded as resource rent (Mikesell 1989). If resource rent is zero, the resource contributes nothing to social output since the labor, capital, and management included in the social costs could produce the same value output in another project without natural resources.

However, for the project to satisfy the condition of sustainability, the resource rent must be at least equal to the resource depletion caused directly or indirectly by construction and operation of the project. If the expected NPSV adjusted for resource depletion were zero, the resource would contribute nothing to net revenue by being used in the project, and it could probably do better than that by simply being left undeveloped. This would be true of a wilderness area that could be used by fishermen and hikers as an alternative to harvesting the timber with a zero or negative NPSV. Also, the alternative of leaving the resource undisturbed would have the additional value of reversibility. When resources are not disturbed they can always be developed at some time in the future when the need for the products of the project is greater. This value is in addition to the possible amenities yielded by resources left in their natural state. Ideally, the use of resources that provides the maximum expected NPSV should be supported. Frequently, that use is simply leaving the resource in an undeveloped state.

It is sometimes argued that accounting for resource depletion as a social cost is impractical because there are no reliable data. I reject this argument for two reasons. First, environmental economists have formulated methods for estimating a wide range of nonmarket costs, including damage to health, rivers and lakes, forest ecosystems, wilderness amenities, and wildlife. Estimates of the value of resource depletion have been made by Repetto and Magrath (1988) and others, and research staffs of the MDBs are in a good position to provide data for natural resource accounting. Second, it is better to have someone acquainted with the environmental aspects of a project estimate the social costs than to ignore them.

Notes

1. The World Bank usually uses an internal rate of return of 12 percent as the minimum acceptable rate.

2. This condition is consistent with the concept of sustainability put forward by the Brundtland Commission (1987). For alternative approaches to the sustainability criterion, see Toman and Crosson (1991).

3. This analysis is adapted from El Serafy (1989, 1991).

4. The present value of R per year for n years equals

$$\frac{R\left(1 - \dfrac{1}{(1+r)^n}\right)}{r} = \frac{R - \dfrac{R}{(1+r)^n}}{r} = \frac{X}{r}$$

References

El Serafy, S. "The Proper Calculation of Income from Depletable Natural Resources." In *Environmental Accounting for Sustainable Development*, edited by Y. Ahmad, S. El Serafy, and E. Lutz. Washington, D.C.: World Bank, 1989.

———. "Depletable Resources: Fixed Capital or Inventories?" Paper presented at the Conference of the International Association for Research in Income and Wealth on Environmental Accounting, Baden, Austria, 27–31 May 1991.

Mikesell, R. F. "Depletable Resources, Discounting and Intergenerational Equity." *Resources Policy*, December 1989: 292–96.

Repetto, R., and W. B. Magrath. *Natural Resources Accounting.* Washington, D.C.: World Resources Institute, 1988.

Toman, M. A., and P. Crosson. "Economics and 'Sustainability': Balancing Tradeoffs and Imperatives." Washington, D.C.: Resources for the Future, January 1991. Mimeo.

World Commission on Environment and Development. "Our Common Future" (The Brundtland Report). Chapter 2. Oxford: Oxford University Press, 1987.

7

Sustainable Development: The Role of Investment

Bernd von Droste and Peter Dogsé

Investment, in all its different forms, shapes our lives as well as that of generations to come. Investments in education, science, technology, culture, and communications, for example, continue to have crucial impacts on welfare. In many cases, today's resource degradation is a function of earlier investment decisions about the scale and quality of consumption and production. This calls for increased understanding of investment processes for improved management of manmade and natural capital.

Rapidly increasing environmental costs prompt scientists and economists to warn that limits are being reached (see Chapter 1) and challenges the maxim that continued economic growth leads to increased global welfare (see Chapter 4). To many observers a discussion about limits—for example, to economic growth—might be seen as an academic exercise in a world where so many basic needs are still unmet. Taking these warnings seriously, however, we believe that the question has important implications, which have to be considered by development planners in all parts of the world.

That being said, this chapter is mainly directed toward the North, which is not only primarily responsible for the present situation, but which has many of the resources needed to invest in development that "meets the needs of the present without compromising the ability of future generations to meet their own needs," as noted in the Brundtland Report. Based on the relationship of environmental quality, economic performance, and social welfare, it is now evident that sustainable development demands that larger investments be directed toward the environmental sector for protection and restoration of the productive and assimilative capacity of natural capital.

Increased investments will not only be made for adapting to environmental limits, but also for shifting them. Investments in modern biotechnology research and production are an important example of the latter, which pose challenges with far-reaching environmental and socioeconomic consequences, not the least in the South. It is by influencing today's long-term investment decisions, in areas such as biotechnology and renewable energy, that the policy- and decision-making community will have the largest impact on the international community's sustainable development efforts.

Why Do Investments Go Wrong?

Policy-makers tend to underestimate the value of environmental investments because of: time lags (environmental costs and benefits often take time to develop, but political mandates are usually short); practical difficulties in the evaluation of environmental benefits and costs; the transboundary nature of several environmental externalities, making identification of national responsibilities and domestic solutions ambiguous without coordinated international efforts; and high discount rates (short-term time preferences). Furthermore, private investors are often discouraged to make long-term investments in natural capital due to the public-good character of such assets, the lack of property rights arrangements, making the benefits from such investments difficult to secure. Instead, they favor investments in activities that generate income more quickly.

Sustainable development implies, however, that investment processes are not only understood and managed for monetary returns, but that nonmonetary factors (for example, social, cultural, and ecological realities) also be considered (Young and Ishwaran 1989). This means that the value of environmental services and goods must be estimated and incorporated in the decision-making process. The failure of traditional systems of national accounts in this respect is becoming recognized, and considerable work is being undertaken to develop accounting methods that include depreciation (as well as increases) of environmental capital assets and that subtract defensive expenditures[1] from national income (Ahmad, El Serafy, and Lutz 1989; see also Chapter 5).

In the same way that policy- and decision-makers consult macroeconomic indicators (inflation, "growth," exchange rates, and unemployment figures), they should also be provided with environmental indicators and models illustrating the state of the environment and its impact on the economy, as well as the relationship between economic activity and resource degradation. As it stands now, development models frequently ignore the direct and indirect value of natural capital, both in the economic growth process and in sustaining human welfare. Of course, the availability of such models might be limited, but enough data exist on which decisions could and should be made (Costanza 1990).

Due to the above factors and the increased scale of human activity, there is now a long list of environmental priorities requiring large-scale investment, ranging from the atmosphere (to reduce emissions of greenhouse gases and ozone-layer-depleting chemicals) to local conservation of biological and genetic diversity. The list is so impressive that authors such as Herman E. Daly conclude that since the productivity of manmade capital is becoming more and more constrained by the decreasing supply and quality of complementary natural capital, we are now in an era when "investment must shift from manmade capital accumulation toward natural capital preservation and restoration" (see Chapter 2).

Investment Necessary in the Short Term

The economic rationality behind increased natural capital investments becomes apparent when we look at some costs and benefits involved. The worldwide lack of investment in soil protection is one practical example. Due to various short-term, income-generating activities (for example, deforestation, intensive agriculture, and irrigation), 25 billion tons of soil are lost worldwide each year. It is calculated that over a twenty-year period, U.S. $4.5 billion-per-year investment in soil protection would reduce the annual cost of lost agricultural production by U.S. $26 billion (Lazarus 1990). In addition, increased soil investments would also produce benefits outside the agricultural sector (for example, reducing sedimentation in many hydroelectric dams, improving water quality, and increasing fish catches).[2]

Another example is current damage in European forests from air pollution, which is conservatively estimated at U.S. $30 billion per year. Although the European countries have agreed to spend some U.S. $9 billion per year to reduce air pollution, additional investments are calculated to be cost-effective (International Institute for Applied Systems Analysis 1990).

In spite of the fact that today's investments are often smaller than what is necessary, the amounts spent on mitigating environmental costs will likely fund a new industrial sector for pollution control and waste management in the near future. In the Organization for Economic Cooperation and Development (OECD) countries, some 9 billion tonnes of wastes were produced in 1990, including nearly 1500 tonnes of industrial wastes (of which 300 million tonnes were hazardous) and 420 million tonnes of municipal wastes (OECD 1991). In 1992, estimates indicate that the pollution control industry in Western Europe alone is a U.S. $120 billion-per-year business. By 1994 more than U.S. $200 billion might have to be spent annually on clean-up and pollution control in the United States. Increased knowledge and industrial efficiency in these fields are welcomed, but it is unfortunate that so many companies and employees will depend on continued environmental degradation for their income. The urgent need for a massively expanded waste treatment and pollution control sector reflects historical lack of infrastructure investments and calls for substantially increased efforts toward finding environmentally sound production processes and products.

With the increasing scarcity of natural capital goods and services, investments in the rehabilitation of degraded ecosystems have become all the more important. Not only can rehabilitated natural capital assets produce significant incomes, they often also constitute the best way to protect remaining natural areas from degradation. Since the time and investment necessary to undertake restoration activities increase significantly with the increasing level of ecosystem degradation, rapid action is essential.

Approximately 80 percent of the potentially productive arid and semiarid lands worldwide (representing 35 percent of the earth's land surface) suffered from moderate to severe desertification in the early 1980s, due primarily to poor land management (Dregne 1983). In many arid and semiarid areas, the natural resource base is, therefore, no longer able to sustain existing human populations. Due to high population growth rates this will worsen in the near future. In the year 2000 there will be a rural population of at least 40 million in the Sahelian and Sudanian zones of West Africa (calculated from a conservative 2 percent annual population increase). This is 3.7 million people more than what the current crop and livestock production systems of this region can support, or 19.1 million more than what can be sustained by fuel wood, the energy source on which these societies rely (World Bank 1985). Unless these areas are successfully rehabilitated, continued worldwide desertification may leave hundreds of millions of people as environmental refugees (Gregersen, Draper, and Elz 1989; Simon 1991).

Financing Investments in the South and in Eastern Europe

Increasingly aware of environmental values but hampered by severe budget constraints, many developing countries find it difficult to make long-term investments in their natural capital assets, in particular since increased consumption is also seen as a major priority (African Centre for Technology Studies 1990). Their need for additional investment resources can only be evaluated as alarming.[3] Developing countries often argue, for example, that they cannot afford environmentally sound techniques, if less expensive but polluting alternatives exist, and that it is now their turn to benefit from the technologies the industrial world has been using for a long time.

However, as so much of today's technology is not environmentally sustainable, it is therefore not economically sustainable. As the developed world already has produced such large concentrations of environmental toxins, the value of the negative externalities that would be produced by additional emissions is no longer marginal and in many cases no longer external. Developing nations therefore cannot invest in environmentally unsound techniques without facing rising domestic environmental costs, thus reducing the return on the investment and jeopardizing the success of future sustainable development. Several countries in Eastern Europe are striking examples. By pursuing economic growth at the expense of the environment, they now face tremendous ecological damage. The German Institute for Economic Research has estimated that industries in Poland, the former German Democratic Republic, Czechoslovakia, and the European part of the former Soviet Union will need U.S. $200 billion to reverse prior environmental neglect (Cave 1990).

One could argue that the developed world, by using technologies that have accumulated global toxins, to some extent has reduced the option for developing countries to use the same technologies (or any other techniques with the same impacts) because of the risk of potential future environmental catastrophes. Industrial countries should, therefore, be prepared to compensate the developing world for these closed options. This could be done partly by financing sustainable technology investments in developing countries and partly by dramatically cutting back on their own emissions to give space for increased use of environmentally unsound technologies in developing countries without increasing the total global environmental abuse. Indeed, the North has to reduce input growth and waste, using both economic and legal instruments, while at the same time providing the South with capital and sound technologies through various arrangements, such as green funds and debt-for-sustainable-development swaps (Hansen 1989; Dogsé and von Droste 1990).

The Multilateral Fund agreed upon by the contracting parties to the Montreal Protocol to provide developing countries with additional funds for obtaining ozone-friendly technologies and replacements of CFCs, is an important achievement in this direction. The U.S. $160 million fund will expand to U.S. $240 million if China and India—both planning major CFC production increases—eventually ratify the Montreal Protocol. This fund is now part of the U.S. $1.4 billion pilot Global Environment Facility (GEF), which is administered by the World Bank, United Nations Environment Program (UNEP), and United Nations Development Program (UNDP). The GEF funds, however modest in size compared with identified needs (World Resources Institute 1990), are to be used for investments in three additional areas: greenhouse gas emission reductions, conservation of biological and genetic diversity, and protection of international water resources.

Also, the European Bank for Reconstruction and Development (EBRD) has the potential to become an important financier of investments with positive environmental impact. The EBRD's first loan, which was given to Poland for a heating project, is promising. The U.S. $50 million loan (together with a U.S. $20 million World Bank credit) aims at reducing air pollution by switching from coal to gas-fired heat generation and by promoting energy efficiency (*International Herald Tribune* 1991).

Developing nations cannot, however, always rely on industrial nations to develop and transfer appropriate technologies to them. They should be prepared to make part of that investment themselves so as to ensure that technologies fit their economic, cultural, and natural environments. In some cases this will mean that local, small-scale production units are stimulated, which may require that innovative finance approaches first have to be developed. Initiatives such as the Grameen Bank in Bangladesh, which in 1988 operated with 413,000 participants, has shown that it is possible to provide financial support to the rural poor and landless (World Bank 1990). The poor, heavily dependent on the natural environment, frequently have very limited means for making long-term investments in natural capital. Therefore they often have to sacrifice investment for consumption.

Long-term Investments

By underestimating the value of our natural capital, we are now in a situation where more and more resources will have to be spent on restoration, waste disposal, and protection of the natural capital that is left, often without producing any extra gain in welfare. Although the new problems produced by modern economic growth might be soluble, the costs for doing so are unnecessarily high, as many of today's environmental problems should never have been produced in the first place and their costs and the ability to solve them are very far from equally distributed. Sustainable development must, therefore, ensure that scarce resources are invested in research and in the production of processes and systems that not only avoid known problems but also anticipate unknown costs and benefits. This requires realism and vision.

Although we are generally optimistic, the energy sector, central in all discussions on sustainable development, provides several examples of excess investment in research and development of unsustainable processes and lack of investment in renewables. One of the most glaring is the fact that in 1989 the twenty-one member countries of the International Energy Agency (IEA) spent 75 percent of their U.S. $7.3 billion energy research budget on fossil fuels and nuclear energy, but only 7 percent on renewables and 5 percent on energy conservation (see Table 1).

The fact that investments are directed inefficiently might often depend on the institutions responsible for their administration. Institutions that once were efficient in their field of competence and mandate may not adapt rapidly enough to new or evolving demands. Why, for example, is there no United Nations body working on the promotion of energy conservation and renewables when there is one dedicated to the promotion of nuclear power (the International Atomic Energy Agency, IAEA)? The IAEA, which in 1991 had a budget of U.S. $179 million, with U.S. $70 million expected in additional voluntary contributions, has as its major role to monitor nuclear proliferation, but it is also said to actively promote export of nuclear power technology to developing nations. At present, developing countries obtain 40 percent of their energy from renewables and less than 1 percent from nuclear plants (Flavin and Lensen 1990). The creation of a United Nations agency for renewable energy sources and conservation would clearly be justified and should, therefore, be considered by the United Nations Conference on Environment and Development (UNCED).[4]

Existing institutions may reflect historical preferences rather than

Table 1
Energy Research and Development Spending by IEA Governments, 1989

Technology	Amount U.S. $ million	Share (%)
Nuclear Fission	3466	47
Fossil Fuel	1098	15
Nuclear Fusion	883	12
Renewables	498	7
Conservation	367	5
Other	1039	14
Total	7351	100

Source: Flavin and Lensen (1990).

modern needs, and the interest of "old" organizations in modern sustainability issues might be larger than their ability to cope with them. This brings up the whole issue of either establishing new institutions or updating existing ones—a long-term investment in itself.

Limits and Research and Development

The increased visibility of environmental degradation costs has resulted in more scientists warning that various limits are being reached, or have already been exceeded, and more economists are challenging the traditional wisdom that continued economic growth leads to increased welfare (see Chapter 1). On the question of limits, although there is scientific consensus regarding certain physical constraints and hazards to economic growth, we do not have consensus regarding our possibilities to meet these challenges or on the economic consequences of crossing these limits. No irreversible event is, from an anthropocentric point of view, worse than our subjective, and dynamic, evaluation of it.

Doubtless, humanity will also try to control future limits as has happened throughout history. This will certainly include increasingly sophisticated manipulation of biological and physical processes, ranging from microcosmos to the atmosphere, if not beyond. Efforts will be made to increase the photosynthetic capacities in plants by cell engineering; rice, maize, and pulse genomes might be completely mapped and genetic diseases cured; agricultural soils and oceans might be turned into carbon sinks to mitigate the greenhouse effect; etc. But we must recognize that these are still unknown technologies that will probably bring unknown side effects (just as did leaded gasoline, asbestos, CFCs, etc.).

Shifting Biological Limits

The economic forces boosting biological productivity are already immense (see Table 2), and it would be naive to think that major (public and private) investments will not be made for such purposes. Allocation and management of investment capital going into modern biotechnology research and production is—because of its promises, risks, and socioeconomic consequences—a key area of concern in sustainability discussions.[5]

Table 2
Examples of Commercial Economic Benefits from Conventional Crop Breeding

Potential Benefits (U.S. $ per year)	Commercial Beneficiary	"Improvement"
4.4 billion	Worldwide	Crossing of a perennial Mexican corn able to grow in marginal soils at high altitudes and that is resistant to seven major corn diseases with modern annual corn varieties
3.5 billion	Asia	Improved production by incorporating dwarfism into wheat and rice
160 million	U.S.A.	A single gene from an Ethiopian barley plant introduced to commercial barley crops protects them from yellow dwarf virus

Source: United Nations Environment Program (1990).

Advanced knowledge about how gene expression works is now used in increased food and energy production, new medicines, raw materials, and in improved environmental management. There is also great interest from the defense industry. Increased knowledge about manipulation of biological processes is, as with knowledge in general, a doubled-edged sword: the key to control is also the key to destruction. Because of the huge stakes and the vast numbers of actors involved in biotechnology, the question of moral discipline poses major concerns.

Biotechnology applications can speed up or slow down entropy increases, in both unsustainable and sustainable processes, in a more equitable or less equitable international order. The particular responsibilities now facing national and international policy- and decision-makers in the field of biotechnology are among the most urgent and difficult on their agenda.

Biotechnology is seen as a major chance for developing tropical countries to gain from their rich biological and genetic diversity. Unless developing countries become much better prepared to influence and control present and future investments in biotechnology research and production, however, they are in serious difficulty, with far-reaching consequences for their economic and environmental sustainability. The risk (from the South's perspective) is that additional comparative advantages will be given to the North, making it impossible for the South to compete in the production of various agricultural goods for which there is, or will be, a large demand and high value-added potential.

By using subsidies, trade barriers, and environmentally unsustainable production technologies, the North already produces agricultural surpluses that suppress world market prices and production in the South. Given that the North is not prepared to forego some of its present market control, which seriously inhibits development efforts in the South, it may not hesitate to strengthen its position further. Although perhaps not primarily as a consequence of North-South but North-North competition, the North will most likely take the lead in investing in natural capital using low-cost genetic "raw materials" from the South. This would be analogous to manmade capital competition where the South in many cases was unable to develop competitive value-added processes (for example, saw mills, paper factories, metal industries, etc.) and fell back on selling natural resources at falling prices.

Small farmers in developing countries may be the largest losers in such a scenario, since they are least able to undertake and influence investments needed for them to stay competitive, even in domestic markets. The socioeconomic consequences of decreasing economic sustainability on the rural poor, which may force large populations to search for their livelihood in increasingly unsustainable cities, should not be underestimated. This leaves the South with the question of to what extent they actually benefit from so-called "free-trade" and technology transfers—and to consider what measures they eventually can take to improve their own development potential in a situation where international economic competition is so unbalanced in favor of the North.

Time for Action

It will take some ten years for today's investments in research and development of new biotechnology to reap economically significant results. It will then, in many cases, be too late to correct for unwanted side effects and costs. The international community should therefore assess risks, benefits, and costs, as well as their distribution, and seek to control the development of such technology at the earliest possible stage.

Much of the discussion above points to the responsibilities of public sectors as large-scale investors. Since many large biotechnology and energy research investments are made by the private sector, however, the public sector also has the responsibility of influencing private investment.[6] Maurice Strong's statement on the importance of incorporating the private sector into development planning is particularly relevant: "Business is the major engine of development in our society. And, therefore if we can't influence business, we really can't influence development" (Dampier 1982). In particular, this will mean taking the needs of the South into consideration, including elaboration and assessment of how, through legal, economic, and policy arrangements, developing countries can best be strengthened in their research and investment capacities.

Conclusion

Compared with the costs, 0.8 to 1.5 percent of gross domestic product (GDP), industrial countries have received significant benefits from their environmental programs during the last twenty years (OECD 1991). Although natural capital investments made are too low, for those countries who have invested even less, or hope to avoid such investments in the future, the bill will get much higher.

It is, therefore, encouraging to note that public opinion in the United States, Japan, and fourteen European countries now indicates strong support for the environment, even in situations where protection of the environment would reduce economic growth (OECD 1991). Such attitudes are a good basis for building the necessary institutional changes in the industrial world for improved understanding and management of investment capital in relation to existing (and possibly shifted) ecological constraints on economic growth. It is also the best guarantee that innovative financial bodies, such as the GEF, will get increased resources and a mandate to help promote sustainable investment practices in the South.

However, throughout history, although being fully aware of environmental constraints, societies failed to secure a sustainable balance between immediate consumption and long-term natural capital investment and, therefore, eventually collapsed (Ponting 1990). Furthermore, although these societies were constrained by only local or regional environmental limits, today's global limits will require a level of international coordination and cooperation never before necessary in the history of humankind.

Acknowledgments

The authors are indebted to Robert Goodland, Ignacy Sachs, and Dana Silk for valuable comments on an earlier version of this chapter.

Notes

1. Costs necessary to maintain (defend) a certain level of welfare, which, due to unwanted side effects of consumption and production, such as pollution, threatens to fall.

2. It has been estimated that siltation of dams feeding hydropower turbines involves a loss of some 148,000 gigawatt hours, which at U.S. $15 per barrel would cost some U.S. $4 billion per year to replace using oil-fired thermal generation (Pearce 1987).

3. The World Resources Institute (WRI) has estimated that the Third World's unmet financial needs for maintaining its natural resources as "the basis for meeting the needs for current and future generations" amounts to U.S. $20 billion to $50 billion per year over the next decade (WRI 1990).

4. The UNEP Collaborating Centre on Energy and Environment linked to the Risoe National Laboratory in Denmark, which was opened on 1 October 1990, may be a good starting point toward this end.

5. Biotechnology has been defined as "the application of biological systems and organisms to scientific, industrial, agricultural, health, and environment processes and uses." "Organisms" includes animals, plants, and microbes. "New" biotechnology refers to the use of cell fusion, cell and tissue culture, recombinant DNA, and novel bioprocessing methods. "Old," or classical, biotechnology refers to the use of microbes for baking, brewing, or other fermentation processes, or selective breeding in agriculture and animal husbandry (Giddings and Persley 1990).

6. In 1987, total research and development investment in agricultural biotechnology was estimated at U.S. $900 million, of which more than 60 percent was in the private sector (Giddings and Persley 1990).

References

African Centre for Technology Studies. *The Nairobi Declaration on Climatic Change.* International Conference on Global Warming and Climate Change: Africa Perspectives (2–4 May 1990). Nairobi: African Centre for Technology Studies, 1990.

Ahmad, Y., S. El Serafy, and E. Lutz, eds. *Environmental Accounting for Sustainable Development.* Washington, D.C.: World Bank, 1989.

Cave, S. "Cleaning up Eastern Europe." *Our Planet* 2(2)(1990): 4–7.

Costanza, R. "Ecological Economics as a Framework for Developing Sustainable National Policies." In *Towards an Ecological Sustainable Economy*, edited by B. Aniansson and U. Svedin. Report from a Policy Seminar, in Stockholm, Sweden, 3–4 January 1990, arranged by the Swedish Council for Planning and Coordination of Research on behalf of the Environmental Advisory Council of the Swedish Government. Stockholm: FRN Rapport 90:6, 1990.

Dampier, W. "Strong Assesses the Decade Since Stockholm." In "Synopsis: Ten Years After Stockholm: A Decade of Environmental Debate." *Ambio* 11(4)(1982): 229–31.

Dogsé, P., and B. von Droste. "Debt-for-Nature Exchanges and Biosphere Reserves: Experiences and Potential. *MAB Digest* no. 6. Paris: UNESCO, 1990.

Dregne, H. E. "Desertification of Arid Lands." In vol. 3 of *Advances in Desert and Arid Land Technology and Development*. New York: Harwood Academic Publishers, 1983.

Flavin, C., and N. Lensen. "Beyond the Petroleum Age: Designing a Solar Economy." Worldwatch Paper No. 100. Washington, D.C.: Worldwatch Institute, 1990.

Giddings, L. V., and G. Persley. "Biotechnology and Biodiversity." Study prepared for United Nations Environment Program. UNEP/Bio.Div./SWGB. 1/3, mimeo. 12 October 1990.

Gregersen, H., S. Draper, and D. Elz, eds. *People and Trees: The Role of Social Forestry in Sustainable Development*. Washington, D.C.: World Bank, 1989.

Hansen, S. "Debt for Nature Swaps—Overview and Discussion of Key Issues." *Ecological Economics* 1(1)(1989): 77–93.

International Herald Tribune. "European Development Bank Makes First Loan." *International Herald Tribune*, 22 June 1991, p. 13.

International Institute for Applied Systems Analysis. "Comprehensive Study of European Forests Assesses Damage and Economic Losses from Air Pollution." News release, 5 December 1990.

Lazarus, D. S. "Save our Soils." *Our Planet* 2(4)(1990).

Organization for Economic Cooperation and Development. *The State of the Environment*. Paris: OCED, 1991.

Pearce, D. "Economic Values and the Natural Environment." *University College London Discussion Papers in Economics* 87(8): 1–20.

Ponting, C. "Historical Perspectives on Sustainable Development." *Environment* 32(9)(1990): 15–28.

Simon, B. "Report Predicts Flood of 'Environmental Refugees.' " *Financial Times*, 25 June 1991, p. 6.

United Nations Environment Program. "Note by UNEP on Basic Issues With Respect to Biotechnology and Conservation of Biological Diversity." *Ad hoc* Working Group of Experts on Biological Diversity, Subworking Group on Biotechnology, United Nations Environment Program, Nairobi, 14–16 November 1990. UNEP/Bio.Div./SWGB.1/2, mimeo. 15 October 1990, Annex 2.

World Bank, *Desertification in Sahelian and Sudanian Zones in West Africa.* Washington, D.C.: World Bank, 1985.

World Bank. *World Development Report 1990.* Washington, D.C.: World Bank, 1990.

World Resources Institute. *Natural Endowments: Financing Resource Conservation for Development.* Washington, D.C.: World Resources Institute, 1990.

Young, M., and N. Ishwaran, eds. "Human Investment and Resource Use: A New Research Orientation at the Environment/Economic Interface." *MAB Digest* no. 2. Paris: UNESCO, 1989.

The Ecological Economics
of Sustainability:
Investing in Natural Capital

Robert Costanza

An Ecological Economic World View

To achieve global sustainability, we need to stop thinking of ecological and economic goals as being in conflict. Economic systems are dependent on their ecological life-support systems, and we must realize that fact and incorporate it into our thinking and actions at a very basic level if we are to sustain our global household. A house divided against itself cannot long stand.

To achieve sustainability we must develop an *ecological economics* that goes well beyond the conventional disciplines of ecology and economics to a truly integrative synthesis (Costanza 1991).

Figure 1 illustrates one aspect of the relationship between ecological economics and the conventional approaches: the domains of the different subdisciplines. The upper left box represents the domain of "conventional" economics, the interactions of economic sectors (such as mining, manufacturing, and households) with one another. The domain of "conventional" ecology, in the lower right box, represents the interactions of ecosystems and their components with one another. The lower left box represents the inputs from ecological sectors to economic sectors. This is the usual domain of resource economics and environmental impact analysis: the use of renewable and nonrenew-

106

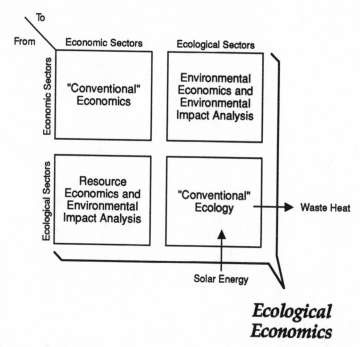

Ecological Economics

Figure 1. The domains of conventional economics, conventional ecology, environmental and resource economics, and ecological economics.

able natural resources by the economy. The upper right box represents the "use" by ecological sectors of economic "products." The products of interest in this box are usually unwanted by-products of production and the ultimate wastes from consumption. This is the usual domain of environmental economics and environmental impact analysis: pollution and its mitigation, prevention, and mediation. Ecological economics encompasses and transcends these disciplinary boundaries. Ecological economics sees the human economy as part of a larger whole. Its domain is the entire web of interactions between economic and ecological sectors.

Table 1 presents some of the other major differences between ecological economics (EE) and conventional economics (CEcon) and conventional ecology (CEcol). The basic world view of CEcon is one in which

Table 1
Comparison of "Conventional" Economics and Ecology with Ecological Economics

	"Conventional" Economics	"Conventional" Ecology	Ecological Economics
Basic World View	*Mechanistic, Static, Atomistic* Individual taxes and preferences are taken as given and the dominant force. The resource base is viewed as essentially limitless due to technical progress and infinite substitutability.	*Evolutionary, Atomistic* Evolution acting at the genetic level is viewed as the dominant force. The resource base is limited. Humans are just another species but are rarely studied.	*Dynamic, Systems, Evolutionary* Human preferences, understanding, technology, and organization coevolve to reflect broad ecological opportunities and constraints. Humans are responsible for understanding their role in the larger system and managing it for sustainability.
Time Frame	*Short* 50 years maximum; 1 to 4 years.	*Multiscale* Days to eons, but time scales often define noncommunicating subdisciplines.	*Multiscale* Days to eons, multiscale synthesis.
Space Frame	*Local to International* Framework invariant at increasing spatial scale; basic units change from individuals to firms to countries.	*Local to Regional* Most research has focused on relatively small research sites in single ecosystems, but larger scales becoming more important recently.	*Local to Global* Hierarchy of scales.

	Humans Only	Nonhumans Only	Whole Ecosystem, Including Humans
Species Frame	Plants and animals only rarely included for contributary value.	Attempts to find "pristine" ecosystems untouched by humans.	Acknowledges interconnections between humans and rest of nature.
Primary Macro Goal	Growth of National Economy	Survival of Species	Sustainability of Ecological Economic System
Primary Micro Goal	Maximum Profits (Firms) Maximum Utility (Individuals) All agents following micro goals leads to macro goal being fulfilled. External costs and benefits given lip service but usually ignored.	Maximum Reproductive Success All agents following micro goals leads to macro goal being fulfilled.	Must Be Adjusted to Reflect System Goals Social organization and cultural institutions at higher levels of the space/time hierarchy ameliorate conflicts produced by myopic pursuit of micro goals at lower levels, and vice versa.
Assumptions About Technical Progress	Very Optimistic	Pessimistic or No Opinion	Prudently Skeptical
Academic Stance	Disciplinary Monistic, focus on mathematical tools.	Disciplinary More pluralistic than economics, but still focused on tools and techniques. Few rewards for comprehensive, integrative work.	Transdisciplinary Pluralistic, focus on problems.

individual human consumers are the central figures. Their tastes and preferences are taken as given and are the dominant, determining force. The resource base is viewed as essentially limitless due to technical progress and infinite substitutability. EE takes a more holistic view, with humans as one component (albeit a very important one) in the overall system. Human preferences, understanding, technology, and cultural organization all coevolve to reflect broad ecological opportunities and constraints. Humans have a special place in the system because they are responsible for understanding their own role in the larger system and managing it for sustainability. This basic world view is similar to that of CEcol, in which the resource base is viewed as limited and humans are just another (albeit seldom studied) species. But EE differs from CEcol in the importance it gives to humans as a species and its emphasis on the mutual importance of cultural and biological evolution.

We must acknowledge that the human system is a subsystem within the larger ecological system. This implies not only a relationship of interdependence, but ultimately a relation of dependence of the subsystem on the larger parent system. The first questions to ask about a subsystem are: how big is it relative to the total system? how big can it be? and how big should it be? These questions of scale are only now beginning to be asked (Daly and Cobb 1989).

The presumed goals of the systems under study are also quite distinct, especially at the macro level. The macro goal of EE is sustainability of the combined ecological economic system. CEcol's macro goal of species survival is similar to sustainability but is generally confined to a single species and not the whole system. CEcon emphasizes growth rather than sustainability at the macro level. At the micro level, EE is unique in acknowledging the two-way linkages between scales, rather than the one-way view of the conventional sciences in which all macro behavior is the simple aggregation of micro behavior. In EE, social organization and cultural institutions at higher levels of the space/time hierarchy ameliorate conflicts produced by myopic pursuit of micro goals at lower levels, and vice versa.

Perhaps the key distinctions between EE and the conventional sciences lie in their academic stances and their assumptions about technical progress. As already noted, EE is transdisciplinary, pluralistic, integrative, and more focused on problems than on tools.

CEcon is very optimistic about the ability of technology ultimately to remove all resource constraints to continued economic growth. CEcol has very little to say directly about technology, since it tends to ignore humans altogether. But to the extent that it has an opinion, it would be pessimistic about technology's ability to remove resource constraints, because all other existing natural ecosystems that do not include humans are observed to be resource-limited. EE is prudently skeptical in this regard. Given our high level of uncertainty about this issue, it is irrational to *bank on* technology's ability to remove resource constraints. If we do, and we are wrong, then the result is disastrous, irreversible destruction of our resource base and civilization itself. For the time being, at least, we should assume that technology will *not* be able to remove resource constraints. If it does, we can be pleasantly surprised. If it does not, we are still left with a sustainable system. EE assumes this prudently skeptical stance on technical progress.

Sustainability: Maintaining Our Global Life-Support System

While acknowledging that the sustainability concept requires much additional research, we can offer the following working definition. Sustainability is a relationship between dynamic human economic systems and larger dynamic, but normally slower-changing, ecological systems in which: (1) human life can continue indefinitely; (2) human individuals can flourish; (3) human cultures can develop; but in which (4) the effects of human activities remain within bounds, so as not to destroy the diversity, complexity, and function of the ecological life-support system.

Sustainability does not imply a static, much less a stagnant, economy, but we must be careful to distinguish between *growth* and *development*, as specified in the introduction to this book. Economic growth, which is an increase in quantity, cannot be sustainable indefinitely on a finite planet. Economic development, which is an improvement in the quality of life without necessarily causing an increase in the quantity of resources consumed, may be sustainable. Sustainable growth is an impossibility. Sustainable development must become our primary long-term policy goal.

The most obvious danger of ignoring the role of nature in economics is that nature is the economy's life-support system, and by ignoring it we may inadvertently damage it beyond its ability to repair itself. Indeed, there is much evidence that we have already done so (see Chapter 1). Current economic systems do not *inherently* incorporate any concern about the sustainability of our natural life-support system and the economies that depend on it (Costanza and Daly 1987). In an important sense, sustainability is merely justice with respect to future generations. This includes future generations of other species, even though our main interest may be in our own species.

Sustainability has been variously construed (Pezzey 1989; World Commission on Environment and Development 1987), but a useful definition is the amount of consumption that can be continued indefinitely without degrading capital stocks—including natural capital stocks. In a business, capital stock includes long-term assets such as buildings and machinery that serve as the means of production. Natural capital is the soil and atmospheric structure, plant and animal biomass, etc., that, taken together, forms the basis of all ecosystems. This natural capital stock uses primary inputs (sunlight) to produce the range of ecosystem services and physical natural resource flows. Examples of natural capital include forests, fish populations, and petroleum deposits. The natural resource flows yielded by these natural capital stocks are, respectively, cut timber, caught fish, and pumped crude oil. We have now entered a new era in which the limiting factor in development is no longer manmade capital but remaining natural capital. Timber is limited by remaining forests, not saw mill capacity; fish catch is limited by fish populations, not by fishing boats; crude oil is limited by remaining petroleum deposits, not by pumping and drilling capacity. Most economists view natural and manmade capital as substitutes rather than complements. Consequently, neither factor can be limiting. Only if factors are complementary can one be limiting. Ecological economists see manmade and natural capital as fundamentally complementary and therefore emphasize the importance of limiting factors and changes in the pattern of scarcity. This is a fundamental difference that needs to be reconciled through debate such as presented in this book.

To implement sustainability, all projects should meet the following criteria. For renewable resources, the rate of harvest should not exceed the rate of regeneration (sustainable yield), and the rates of waste generation from projects should not exceed the assimilative capacity of the environment (sustainable waste disposal). For nonrenewable resources, the rates of waste generation from projects shall not exceed the assimilative capacity of the environment, and the depletion of the nonrenewable resources should require comparable development of renewable substitutes for those resources. These are safe, minimum sustainability standards; once these are met, projects should be selected that have the highest rates of return based on other, more traditional economic criteria.

Maintaining and Investing in Natural Capital to Ensure Sustainability

A minimum necessary condition for sustainability is the maintenance of the total natural capital stock at or above the current level. While a lower stock of natural capital may be sustainable, given our uncertainty and the dire consequences of guessing wrong, it is best to at least provisionally assume that we are at or below the range of sustainable stock levels and allow no further decline in natural capital. This "constancy of total natural capital" rule can thus be seen as a prudent minimum condition for ensuring sustainability, to be abandoned only when solid evidence to the contrary can be offered. In fact, we should begin the process of reinvesting in natural capital stocks to bring them back to safe minimum standards. There is disagreement between technological optimists (who see technical progress eliminating all resource constraints to growth and development) and technological skeptics (who do not see as much scope for this approach and fear irreversible use of resources and damage to natural capital). By limiting total system natural capital at current levels (preferably by using higher severance and consumption taxes), we can satisfy both the skeptics (since resources will be conserved for future generations) and the optimists (since this will raise the price of natural capital resources and more rapidly induce the technical change they predict). By limiting physical growth, only development is allowed, and this may proceed without endangering sustainability.

Policy Instruments: Environmental Assurance Bonding

We need to explore promising alternatives to our current command and control environmental management systems and to modify existing government agencies and other institutions accordingly. The enormous uncertainty about local and transnational environmental impacts must be incorporated into decision-making. We also must better understand the sociological, cultural, and political criteria for acceptance or rejection of policy instruments.

One example of an innovative policy instrument currently being studied is a flexible environmental assurance bonding system designed to incorporate environmental criteria and uncertainty into the market system and to induce positive environmental technological innovation (Perrings 1989; Costanza and Perrings 1990).

In addition to being directly charged for known environmental damages, a company would be required to post an assurance bond equal to the current best estimate of the largest potential future environmental damages; the money would be kept in an interest-bearing escrow account. After the project, the bond (plus a portion of the interest) would be returned if the firm could show that the suspected damages had not occurred or would not occur. If they did, the bond would be used to rehabilitate or repair the environment and to compensate injured parties. Thus, the burden of proof would be shifted from the public to the resource user, and a strong economic incentive would be provided to research the true costs of environmentally damaging activities and to develop cost-effective pollution control technologies. This is an extension of the "polluter pays" principle to "the polluter pays for uncertainty as well." Other innovative policy instruments include tradeable pollution and depletion quotas at both national and international levels. Also worthy of mention is the newly emerging Global Environment Facility, which will provide concessionary funds for investments that reduce global externalities.

Economic Incentives: Linking Revenues and Uses

We should implement fees on the destructive use of natural capital in order to promote more efficient use and ease up on income taxes, especially on low incomes, in the interest of equity. Fees, taxes, and subsidies should be used to change the prices of activities that interfere with sustainability relative to those that are compatible with it. This can be accomplished by using the funds generated to support alternatives to undesirable activities that are being taxed. For example, a tax on all greenhouse gases, with the size of the tax linked to the impact of each gas, could be linked to development of alternatives to fossil fuel. Gasoline tax revenues could be used to support mass transit and bike lanes. Current policies that subsidize environmentally harmful activities should be eliminated. For example, subsidies for virgin material extraction should be discontinued. This will also allow recycling options to compete effectively. Crop subsidies that dramatically increase pesticide and fertilizer use should be eliminated, and forms of positive incentives should also be used. For example, debt-for-nature swaps should be supported and should receive much more funding. We should also offer prestigious prizes for work that increases awareness of or contributes to sustainability issues, such as changes in behavior that develop a culture of maintenance (for example, cars that last for fifty years) or that promote capital and resource-saving improvements (for example, affordable, efficient housing and water supplies).

Ecological Economic Research

While economics has developed many useful tools of analysis, it has not directed these tools toward the thorny questions that arise when considering the concept and implementation of sustainability. In particular, we must better understand preference formation, and especially time preference formation. We also need to understand how individual time preferences and group time preferences may differ, and how the preferences of institutions that will be critical to the success or failure of sustainability are established. We have heretofore paid too little attention to ecological feedbacks. An understanding of these will be critical to the implementation of sustainability goals. We need to concentrate on the valuation of important nonmarket goods and services provided by ecosystems (Costanza et al. 1989).

Ecological Economics Education

We need to develop an ecological economics core curriculum and degree-granting programs that embody the skills of both economics and ecology. This implies a curriculum with some blending of physical, chemical, and biological sciences and economics. Within this curriculum quantitative methods are essential, but they should be problem-directed rather than presented as just mathematical tools for their own sake. Experimentation capacity is needed to provide ecological economics with a solid empirical base that is built upon creative and comprehensive theory. We must develop extension programs that can effectively transfer information among disciplines and among nations.

Institutional Changes

Institutions with the flexibility necessary to deal with ecologically sustainable development are lacking. Indeed, many financial institutions are built on the assumption of continuous exponential growth and will face major restructuring in a sustainable economy. Many existing institutions have fragmented mandates and policies and often have not optimally utilized market and nonmarket forces to resolve environmental problems. They have also conducted inadequate cost-benefit analyses by not incorporating ecological costs; used short-term planning horizons; inappropriately assigned property rights (public and private) to resources; and not made appropriate use of incentives.

There is a lack of awareness and education about sustainability, the environment, and causes of environmental degradation. In addition, much environmental knowledge held by indigenous peoples is being lost, as is knowledge of species, particularly in the tropics. Institutions have been slow to respond to new information and shifts in values—for example, threats to biodiversity or rapid changes in communications technologies. Finally, many institutions do not freely share or disseminate information; do not provide public access to decision-making; and do not devote serious attention to determining and representing the wishes of their constituencies.

Many of these problems are a result of the inflexible bureaucratic structure of many modern institutions. Experience (for example, in Japanese industry) has shown that less bureaucratic, more flexible, more peer-to-peer institutional structures can be much more efficient and effective. We need to debureaucratize institutions so that they can effectively respond to the coming challenges of achieving sustainability.

References

Costanza, R., ed. *Ecological Economics: The Science and Management of Sustainability.* New York: Columbia University Press, 1991.

Costanza, R., and H. E. Daly. "Toward an Ecological Economics." *Ecological Modeling* 38 (1987): 1–7.

Costanza, R., S. C. Farber, and J. Maxwell. "The Valuation and Management of Wetland Ecosystems. *Ecological Economics* 1 (1989): 335–61.

Costanza, R., and C. H. Perrings. "A Flexible Assurance Bonding System for Improved Environmental Management." *Ecological Economics* 2 (1990): 57–76.

Daly, H. E., and J. B. Cobb. *For the Common Good: Redirecting the Economy Toward Community, the Environment, and a Sustainable Future.* Boston: Beacon Press, 1989.

Perrings, C. "Environmental Bonds and the Incentive to Research in Activities Involving Uncertain Future Effects." *Ecological Economics* 1 (1989): 95–110.

Pezzey, J. *Economic Analysis of Sustainable Growth and Sustainable Development.* Environment Department Working Paper 15. Washington, D.C.: World Bank, 1989.

World Commission on Environment and Development. "Our Common Future" (The Brundtland Report). Oxford: Oxford University Press, 1987.

9

From Growth to Sustainable Development

Lester R. Brown, Sandra Postel, and Christopher Flavin

For much of this century, economic debates have focused on whether capitalism or socialism is the best way to organize a modern industrial economy. That argument now seems to be over, as the nations of Eastern Europe move swiftly toward market mechanisms and as the economy of the former Soviet Union teeters on the brink of collapse. Yet even before the political dust settles from these transformations, a new, more fundamental question has arisen: How can we design a vibrant economy that does not destroy the natural resources and environmental systems on which it depends?

The vast scale and rapid growth of the U.S. $20 trillion global economy are hailed as great achievements of our time. But as the pace of environmental deterioration quickens, the consequences of failing to bridge the gap between the workings of economic systems and natural ones are becoming all too clear.[1]

Redirecting the global economy toward environmental sustainability requires fundamental reforms at both the international and national levels. In an age when tropical deforestation in one country reduces the entire earth's biological richness, when chemicals released on one continent can lead to skin cancer on another, and when CO_2 emissions anywhere hasten climate change everywhere, economic policy-making is no longer exclusively a national concern.

Greatly lessening the developing world's debt burden is a prerequisite for an environmentally sustainable world economy. By 1989, the Third World's external debt stood at U.S. $1.2 trillion, 44 percent of its collective gross national product (GNP). In some countries, the figure was far higher—140 percent in Egypt and Zaire and a staggering 400 percent in Mozambique. Developing nations paid U.S. $77 billion in interest on their debts that year and repaid U.S. $85 billion worth of principal. Since about 1984, the traditional flow of capital from developed to the developing countries has been increasingly offset by a flow of interest and dividends in the opposite direction. Preliminary data for all flows, including grants, show a negative flow to the developing countries of U.S. $2.7 billion in 1989, which compares with a positive flow of U.S. $51 billion in 1981.[2]

Lack of capital has made it nearly impossible for developing countries to invest adequately in forest protection, soil conservation, irrigation improvements, more energy-efficient technologies, or pollution control devices. Even worse, growing debts have compelled them to sell off natural resources, often their only source of foreign currency. Like a consumer forced to hock the family heirlooms to pay credit card bills, developing countries are plundering forests, decimating fisheries, and depleting water supplies—regardless of the long-term consequences. Unfortunately, no global pawnbroker is holding on to this inheritance until the world can afford to buy it back.

Reforming foreign assistance is also critical. Very little of the aid money disbursed to developing countries by governments and international lending institutions supports ecologically sound development. The World Bank, the largest single funder, lacks a coherent vision of a sustainable economy, and thus its lending priorities often run counter to the goal of creating one. Bilateral aid agencies, with a few important exceptions, do little better. Moreover, the scale of total lending falls far short of that needed to help the Third World escape from the overlapping traps of poverty, overpopulation, and ecological decline.

Instruments of Economic Reform

At the heart of the dilemma at the national level is the failure of economies to incorporate environmental costs into private decisions, which results in society at large bearing them, often in unanticipated ways. Automobile drivers do not pay the full costs of local air pollution or long-term climate change when they fill their gas tanks, nor do farmers pick up the whole tab for the health and ecological risks of using pesticides.

Many industrial nations now spend 1 to 2 percent of their total economic output on pollution control, and these figures will increase in the years ahead. Such large sums spent on capturing pollutants at the end of the pipe, while necessary, are to some extent a measure of the economy's failure to foster practices that curb pollution at its source. Governments mandate catalytic converters for cars but neglect energy-efficient transport systems that would lessen automobile dependence. They require expensive methods of treating hazardous waste, while doing little to encourage industries to reduce their generation of waste.[3]

Of the many tools governments can use to reorient economic behavior, fiscal policies offer some of the most powerful. In particular, partially replacing income taxes with environmental taxes could greatly speed the transition to an environmentally sustainable economy without necessarily increasing the total tax burden. Designed to make prices better reflect true costs, a comprehensive set of environmental taxes would include, for example, levies on carbon emissions from fossil fuels, hazardous waste, paper produced from virgin pulp, pesticide sales, and groundwater depletion. Shifting the tax base in this way would help ensure that those causing environmental harm pay the price, rather than society as a whole, and thereby encourage more environmentally sound practices.

A Question of Scale

Even if debt is relieved, development aid is restructured, and an array of green taxes are instituted, there remains the vexing problem of the economy's scale. Listening to most economists and politicians, unlimited expansion of the economy seems not only possible but desirable. Political leaders tout growth as the answer to unemployment, poverty, ailing industries, fiscal crises, and myriad other societal ills. To question the wisdom of growth seems almost blasphemous, so ingrained is it in popular thinking about how the world works.

Yet to agree that creating an environmentally sustainable economy is necessary is to acknowledge that limits on some forms of growth are inevitable—in particular the consumption of physical resources. Textbook models often portray the economy as a self-contained system, with money flowing between consumers and businesses in a closed loop. In reality, however, the economy is not isolated. It operates within the boundaries of a global ecosystem with finite capacities to produce fresh water, form new topsoil, and absorb pollution. As a subset of the biosphere, the economy cannot outgrow its physical limits and still remain intact.[4]

With an annual output of U.S. $20 trillion, the global economy now produces in seventeen days what it took an entire year to generate in 1900. Already, economic activity has breached numerous local, regional, and global thresholds, resulting in desertification, acidification of lakes and forests, and the build-up of greenhouse gases. If growth proceeds along the lines of recent decades, it is only a matter of time before global systems collapse under the pressure.[5]

One useful measure of the economy's size relative to the earth's life-supporting capacity is the share of the planet's photosynthetic product now devoted to human activity. "Net primary production" is the amount of solar energy fixed by green plants through photosynthesis minus the energy used by those plants themselves. It is, in essence, the planet's total food resource, the biochemical energy that supports all forms of animal life, from earthworms to humans.

Vitousek and his colleagues estimate that 40 percent of the earth's annual net primary production on land now goes directly to meet human needs or is indirectly used or destroyed by human activity—leaving 60 percent for the millions of other land-based species with which humans share the planet. While it took all of human history to reach this point, the share could double to 80 percent by the year 2030 if current rates of population growth and consumption continue; rising per capita consumption could shorten the doubling time considerably. Along the way, with people usurping an ever larger share of the earth's life-sustaining energy, natural systems will unravel faster. Exactly when vital thresholds will be crossed irreversibly is impossible to say. But as Vitousek and his colleagues state, those "who believe that limits to growth are so distant as to be of no consequence for today's decision makers appear unaware of these biological realities."[6]

Toward Greater Efficiency and Equity

For humanity to avoid the wholesale breakdown of natural systems requires not just a slowing in the expansion of our numbers but a shift from the pursuit of growth to that of sustainable progress—human betterment that does not come at the expense of future generations. The first and easiest phase in the transition is to increase greatly the efficiency with which water, energy, and materials are used, which will allow people's needs to be satisfied with fewer resources and less environmental harm. This shift is already under way, but it is proceeding at a glacial pace compared with what is needed.

One example of the necessary approach is provided by California. Pioneering energy policies there have fostered utility investments in efficiency, causing electricity use per person to decline 0.3 percent between 1978 and 1988, compared with an 11 percent increase in the rest of the United States. Californians suffered no drop in living standards as a result; indeed, their overall welfare improved, since their electricity bills were reduced, and their cooking, lighting, and other electrical needs were met with less sacrifice of air quality.[7]

Producing goods and services as efficiently as possible and with the most environmentally benign technologies available will move societies a long way toward sustainability, but it will not allow them to achieve it. Continuing growth in material consumption—the number of cars and air conditioners, the amount of paper used, and the like—will eventually overwhelm gains from efficiency, causing total resource use (and all the corresponding environmental damage) to rise. A halving of pollution emissions from individual cars, for example, will not result in much improvement in air quality if the total distance driven doubles, as it has in the United States since 1965.[8]

This aspect of the transition from growth to sustainability is thus far more difficult, as it goes to the heart of people's consumption patterns. In poorer countries, simply meeting the basic needs of growing human numbers will require that consumption of water, energy, and forest products increases, even if these resources are used with the utmost efficiency. But the wealthier industrial countries—especially the dozen that have stabilized their population size, including Austria, Germany, Italy, Norway, Sweden, and Switzerland—are in the best position to begin satisfying their needs with no net degradation of the natural resource base. These countries could be the first to benefit from realizing that some growth costs more than it is worth, and that an economy's optimum size is not its maximum size.[9]

Quality over Quantity

GNP becomes an obsolete measure of progress in a society striving to meet people's needs as efficiently as possible and with the least damage to the environment. What counts is not growth in output, but the quality of services rendered. Bicycles and light rail, for instance, are less resource-intensive forms of transportation than automobiles are and contribute less to GNP. But a shift to mass transit and cycling for most passenger trips would enhance urban life by eliminating traffic jams, reducing smog, and making cities safer for pedestrians. GNP would decrease, but overall well-being would increase.[10]

Likewise, investing in water-efficient appliances and irrigation systems instead of building more dams and diversion canals would meet water needs with less harm to the environment. Since massive water projects consume more resources than efficiency investments do, GNP would tend to decline. But quality of life would improve. It becomes clear that striving to boost GNP is often inappropriate and counterproductive. As ecologist and philosopher Garrett Hardin puts it, "For a statesman to try to maximize the GNP is about as sensible as for a composer of music to try to maximize the number of notes in a symphony."[11]

Abandoning growth as an overriding goal does not and must not mean forsaking the poor. Rising incomes and material consumption are essential to improving well-being in much of the Third World. But contrary to what political leaders imply, global economic growth as currently measured is not the solution to poverty. Despite the fivefold rise in world economic output since 1950, 1.2 billion people—more than ever before—live in absolute poverty today. More growth of the sort engineered in recent decades will not save the poor; only strategies to more equitably distribute income and wealth can.[12]

A Higher Social Order

Formidable barriers stand in the way of shifting from growth to real progress as the central goal of economic policy. The vision that growth conjures up of an expanding pie of riches is a powerful and convenient political tool because it allows the tough issues of income inequality and skewed wealth distribution to be avoided. As long as there is growth, there is hope that the lives of the poor can be bettered without sacrifices from the rich. The reality, however, is that achieving an environmentally sustainable global economy is not possible without the fortunate limiting their consumption in order to leave room for the poor to increase theirs.

With the ending of the Cold War and the fading of ideological barriers, an opportunity has opened to build a new world upon the foundations of peace. A sustainable economy represents nothing less than a higher social order—one as concerned with future generations as with our own, and more focused on the health of the planet and the poor than on material acquisitions and military might. While it is a fundamentally new endeavor, with many uncertainties, it is far less risky than continuing with business as usual.

Notes

1. The $20 trillion world economy is a Worldwatch Institute estimate based on 1988 gross world product from Central Intelligence Agency, *Handbook of Economic Statistics, 1989* (Washington, D.C.: Worldwatch Institute, 1989),

with the former Soviet Union and Eastern Europe gross national products extrapolated from P. Marer, *Dollar GNPs of the USSR and Eastern Europe* (Baltimore: Johns Hopkins University Press, 1985), with adjustment to 1990 based on growth rates from International Monetary Fund, *World Economic Outlook* (Washington, D.C.: *IMF*, 1990), and Central Intelligence Agency, *Handbook of Economic Tables, Budget of the United States Government, Fiscal Year 1990* (Washington, D.C.: U.S. Government Printing Office, 1989).

2. World Bank, *World Debt Tables 1989–1990: External Debt of Developing Countries, Vols. I and II* (Washington, D.C.: *World Bank*, 1989); Organization for Economic Cooperation and Development, *Development Cooperation* (Paris: OECD, December 1990), Table 3–1 (p. 123).

3. Organization for Economic Cooperation and Development, *OECD in Figures* (Paris: OECD, 1990); Kit D. Farber and Gary L. Rutlege, "Pollution Abatement and Control Expenditures, 1984–87," *Survey of Current Business* (Washington, D.C.: U.S. Department of Commerce, June 1990).

4. See H. E. Daly, "Towards an Environmental Macroeconomics," paper presented at "The Ecological Economics of Sustainability: Making Local and Short-Term Goals Consistent with Global and Long-Term Goals," International Society for Ecological Economics, Washington, D.C., May 1990; see also P. R. Ehrlich, "The Limits to Substitution: Meta-Resource Depletion and a New Economic-Ecological Paradigm," *Ecological Economics*, no. 1, 1989.

5. The 1900 global world output taken from L. R. Brown and S. Postel, "Thresholds of Change," in *State of the World, 1987*, ed. L. Brown et al. (New York: W. W. Norton, 1987).

6. P. M. Vitousek et al., "Human Appropriation of the Products of Photosynthesis," *BioScience* 34(6)(1986): 368–73; Population Reference Bureau, *1990 World Population Data Sheet* (Washington, D.C.: PRB, 1990).

7. U.S. Department of Energy (DOE) and Energy Information Agency (EIA), *State Energy Data Report, Consumption Estimates, 1960–1988* (Washington, D.C.: DOE/EIA, 1990); DOE and EIA, *Annual Energy Review, 1988* (Washington, D.C.: DOE/EIA, 1988).

8. Total vehicle kilometers for 1965–1970 taken from U.S. Department of Commerce, *Historical Statistics of the United States, Colonial Times to 1970, Bicentennial Edition* (Washington, D.C.: U.S. Department of Commerce, 1975); for 1970–1988 from DOE and EIA, *Annual Energy Review, 1988*, op. cit.

9. Population Reference Bureau, *1990 World Population Data Sheet*, op. cit.

10. See H. Anderson, "Moving Beyond Economism: New Indicators for Culturally Specific, Sustainable Development," in *Redefining Wealth and Pro-*

gress: New Ways to Measure Economic, Social and Environmental Change (New York: The Bootstrap Press, 1989); H. E. Daly and J. B. Cobb, *For the Common Good* (Boston: Beacon Press, 1989).

11. G. Hardin, "Paramount Positions in Ecological Economics," in *Ecological Economics: The Science and Management of Sustainability*, ed. R. Costanza (New York: Columbia University Press, 1991).

12. A. Durning, *Poverty and the Environment: Reversing the Downward Spiral* (Washington, D.C.: Worldwatch Institute, 1989).

10

Ten Reasons Why Northern Income Growth Is Not the Solution to Southern Poverty

Robert Goodland and Herman E. Daly

As Ghana's Ambassador Edward Kufuor, chairman of the Group of 77, noted at a United Nations General Assembly session in 1991, "Those who make $200 a year should not pay so that those who make $10,000 a year can breathe clean air. . . . We are all in the same planetary boat. A few of us travel first class, while most are in steerage. But if the boat sinks we all drown together."

Divergent Views on How to Reduce Southern Poverty

Decreasing Southern poverty is arguably today's main goal of economic development. The two main views on how this can be achieved are not fully compatible. The traditional view, held by most economists and development agencies, is not working well. For example, the Bretton Woods Institutions were in part created because of macroeconomic market failure, both to maintain full employment and to bridge the income gap between rich and poor, and to intermediate between rich countries and poor. Their leadership role, apart from lending,[1] is as purveyors of ideas, as well as of capital, setting the development agenda. Regarding capital, the volume of concessionary lending declines relative to hard loans, while poverty increases.[2] Net negative transfers from South to North[3] show that the current system is not working as well as it should.[4] Regarding ideas, there is profound confusion, which development agencies could help greatly to clarify. Development agencies are not primarily responsible for this situation, but they did not use as much of their considerable potential influence to change the conditions that contributed.

Net transfers from South to North persist because of mature high-interest debt servicing, in spite of higher real interest rates in developing countries (averaging 17 percent during the 1980s; UNDP 1992), compared with the 4 percent rates in Organization for Economic Co-operation and Development (OECD) countries. To avoid negative transfers, more loans are needed just to cover debt service, thereby increasing total debt. The projects the debt supported were not as productive as expected, therefore growth in debtor countries in the aggregate was less than expected. Consequently, this repayment transfer is not made from a larger income made possible by the productivity of the projects financed by the debt. Of course, not all projects were disappointing, but on average, development prescriptions have not worked as well as calculated. This suggests that traditional prescriptions of how the North should help the South merit overhaul.

Of the two opposing views on how to help the South, the traditional view is that rich, Northern, high-consumption societies should consume yet more in order to help the South by providing larger markets. The alternative view is that the North should stabilize its resource consumption and reduce its damage to global life-support systems. Any higher consumption must come from productivity improvements, rather than from increased throughput growth. If natural resources[5] were infinite, then growth would be unreservedly good. Since resources are finite, then more Northern growth inevitably means less room for Southern growth.[6] Productivity improvements must replace throughput growth as the path of progress for the North, and eventually for the South as well.

Traditional View

The North must grow faster to buy ever more resources from the South; otherwise the South will stagnate. Northern income growth translates into more Northern consumerism. Northern foreign exchange paying for imports from the South will indirectly "trickle down" from the southern elites to alleviate poverty.[7] The United Nations Development Program's (UNDP) 1992 Human Development Report outlines the historic discrediting of the "trickle down" theory. The South is supposed to be almost totally dependent on the North and incapable of transforming its own resources into necessities for its own people. It must export natural resources, whose world market prices have, in general, steadily declined over the last few decades. The increased flow of natural resources supports Northern consumerism. These exports are for foreign exchange used partly to import the latest consumer goods for its own elites, who are not content with locally produced basic wage goods. If the economy were unbounded by a finite ecosystem, then this strategy would be possible and could be defended at least as the lesser evil. Although "trickle down" may not be thought the primary means of achieving development, this view is widely held and is espoused by development agencies and orthodox economists.

Alternative View

The North should stabilize its rate of resource consumption to free resources for the South and to free up ecological space as well. The North has to reduce its overuse of global commons. Environmental sink capacity (and, to a lesser extent, environmental source capacity,[8] as noted by Meadows et al. 1974) has been preempted by the North, thus denying as much room for the South. The North can continue to develop but must cease increasing throughput growth. If the expanding global economy is bounded by a finite inexpandible ecosystem (see Figure 1 in Chapter 1), then this view becomes the realistic one, and the traditional view becomes impossible.

Foreign exchange generated by economic development, both from loans and exports, serves the desires of the rich more than the needs of the poor. Developing countries should be more capable of producing necessities for their own people than producing luxuries for their rich. Foreign exchange is needed more for the latter than the former. This minority alternative view is held by Nobel economists Jan Tinbergen and Trygve Haavelmo, along with expectedly many, if not most, members of the International Society for Ecological Economics. Tinbergen and Hueting (1991) hold that "continuing [with the] prevailing growth path is blocking [global] chances for survival," and Hueting (1990) that "What the world needs **least** is an increase in national income," and "the highest priority is to [halt] any further production growth in rich countries." Haavelmo and Hansen (1991) characterize the two views: "Policies for more equality invariably start off with the statement that the standard of the poor should be raised towards the level of the rich. In other words, lifting the bottom rather than lowering the top." The alternative view suggests adding "lowering or at least transforming the top"—that is, reducing Northern throughput growth and decreasing Northern consumerism. Under current dependency arrangements, a sharp Northern recession would hurt the South while being beneficial to the global environment. We advocate loosening such dependency to help prevent damage to the South.[9]

Both the traditional and the alternative views cannot be right. The alternative view leads us to emphasize the following overlapping elements, which together constitute our "ten reasons" why Northern growth is not the answer to Southern poverty.

1. GNP: A Flawed Measure of Human Well-Being

Gross national product (GNP) as conventionally measured can be a misleading guide in two ways. First, GNP has little to do with human welfare, as well demonstrated by the UNDP's 1992 Human Development Report. Second, economic sectors contributing most to GNP are those that are the most environmentally damaging (see below). Although GNP maximization is unreliable for both prudent economic development and prudent environmental management, economic development takes GNP maximization seriously as a general goal or yardstick. This should not condemn economic activity properly directed to pollution abatement, conservation, and reducing waste.

Recent work on environmental accounting by the World Bank (Ahmad, El Serafy, and Lutz 1989), Hueting (1990; and with Bosch and de Boer 1992) and others shows that environmentally benign activities usually contribute a much smaller part to national income than do environmentally malign ones. On the one hand, conventionally mea-

sured environmental damage and its rectification are "good" for GNP-
boosting growth: for example, the *Exxon Valdez* oil spill clean-up
boosted GNP. On the other hand, environmentally benign activities
tend to be less costly than environmentally malign growth and consequently contribute less to GNP.[10] For example, walking, biking, and
mass transit contribute less to GNP than does automobile use; train
travel contributes less than airplane travel; an extra blanket or sweater
less than raising the thermostat; one-child families less than six-child
families; eating legumes less than eating beef; recycling less than
trashing. A reduction of GNP resulting from choosing these benign activities should be encouraged, not resisted.

Therefore, environmental protection is not, as commonly portrayed,
an expensive choice, largely to be chosen when a nation becomes rich
enough to afford such choices. The opposite is true. At the same time,
rectifying environmentally harmful growth is indeed staggeringly expensive: nuclear and toxic clean-ups and greenhouse-effect reversal, for
example. This strengthens the argument for prevention rather than
cure, and for developing countries not repeating the errors of the industrial countries, which passed through environmentally damaging
phases of economic development.

The contrast between Northern and Southern environments is that
much local Northern environmental damage is pollution and hence reversible. For example, the pollution of London's River Thames and the
"pea-soup" smogs of the 1950s have been largely reversed. On the other
hand, most Southern environmental damage is irreversible loss of biodiversity.[11] Irreversible damage cannot be cured; replacement costs are
infinite. The North's unnecessarily expensive "damage the environment, then cure it" approach may be affordable (but imprudent) for the
rich North. But there are no cures for irreversible damage, and the
South cannot afford such an expensive approach to any reversible types
of damage either. The preventive approach is the only possible one for
the South.

2. Importance of Relative Incomes

The traditional view, emphasizing global income growth, will exacerbate inequality while scarcely denting poverty. An annual 3 percent in-

crease in global per capita income translates initially into annual per capita increments of U.S. $633 for the United States, but only U.S. $10 or less for China, India, Bangladesh, and Nigeria, among others. After a decade, the U.S. income will have risen by $7257, whereas such income growth will have raised Ethiopia's income by only $41. Therefore, advocates of the traditional view, prioritizing global income growth, should at least state that an unwanted side effect will be to worsen income disparity. When dealing with market competition for finite resources, relative income is more influential than absolute income in determining whether some individuals are excluded from access to available resources. Since markets need at least some social equity, the traditional view will gradually exclude the poor from domestic and international market economies. We emphasize equity within countries as well as between countries.

3. Differential Utility of Needs and Wants

For Northern consumers, self-evaluated happiness is more a function of relative income than of absolute income. Therefore, since aggregate growth increases absolute but not relative income, it contributes little to actual happiness in the North (Hirsch 1976). So, although our main concern is alleviation of absolute poverty, we recognize that, above the poverty level, relative income is a more important determinant of satisfaction than absolute income. Now that Northern income growth yields sharply declining marginal utility, the Northern countries should question whether raising their incomes will not increase environmental costs faster than it increases production benefits. Raising Northern incomes not only widens the gap between North and South, but may well be reducing Northern welfare absolutely. In the North's choice between consumerism and saving, the quest for relative standing based on visible commodities has biased the North toward consumerism. Less consumerism and more saving in the North could be invested in much-needed poverty alleviation and growth in the South. Production to meet basic human needs produces relatively high utilities, frequently with relatively low environmental costs. Wants or luxuries generate relatively lower utility, often with higher environmental costs.

4. Misplaced Technological Optimism

New technology is often adopted in order to improve productivity, which in turn can raise material standard of living. The impact of a particular technology depends on the nature of the technology, the size of the population deploying it, and the population's level of affluence. In the I = PAT identity, impact equals population times affluence times technology.[12] Accept here as given that world population is projected to double in forty years, and that rich country per capita income (U.S. $18,330) is twenty-three times that of the poor and middle income countries (U.S. $800).[13] Therefore, to raise Southern affluence to today's level of the North (holding both impact and Northern incomes constant) means technology must improve 2 × 23, or 46 times. Since historical technological improvement rates never have exceeded a fraction of the needed forty-six times, it will be exceedingly difficult for poor countries to catch up with rich countries in forty years, even if the North maintains current levels of income. It will be that much more difficult if the South is to catch up with a moving target, as prescribed by the traditional view.

Furthermore, this forty-six-fold increase must be in resource efficiency, not just in capital or labor efficiency. Historically, much of the increase in capital and labor efficiency has been at the expense of resource efficiency. In agriculture, for example, the increase in labor and capital productivity has required an enormous increase in the complementary resource throughputs (energy, fertilizer, biocides, water), whose productivity has *fallen*.

5. The Value of Economic Self-Reliance

The poor can be helped far more, and with much less environmental damage, by a pattern of development that promotes employment in developing countries—as recently advocated by the World Bank's 1990 "World Development Report: Poverty"—rather than by increasing Northern consumption and relying on "trickle down" as advocated by the traditional view. Poverty alleviation requires employment and self-reliance strategies aimed at using local resources to produce for domestic needs. This translates partly into promotion of value-added and domestic processing and partly into employment creation. True, developing countries may initially waste a large fraction of raw materials during processing because of using obsolescent technology commonly transferred to the South. For example, modern saw mills waste considerably less wood than obsolescent saw mills do. But this argues for accelerating transfer of up-to-date technology, rather than the old colonialist approach of exporting raw materials to be more efficiently milled in the North. Such technology is primarily needed in the areas of renewable energy generation and contraceptive methods. Waste prevention, recycling methods, pollution prevention, increased efficiency, methods to reduce material and energy intensity in manufacturing, and low-input, organic, and recycling agriculture also are priorities. Duchin (1992) argues for supplementing technology transfer by the practice of "industrial ecology," life-cycle engineering for reducing pollution.

6. Throughput Growth as a Source of Both Income Growth and of Environmental Damage

If the activities contributing to national income are disaggregated into two components, environmentally friendly (for example, government services except the military, administration, and justice) and environmentally burdening (for example, agriculture and utilities), about one quarter of the activities (measured in labor volume) generates about 65 percent of increases in national income. "Unfortunately, that 25% is precisely the activities which impair the environment" (Hueting, Bosch, and de Boer 1992). Increase in productivity generated by a relatively small part of the economy spreads throughout the whole society via labor supply/demand linkages. For example, a barber's labor volume and real output have not appreciably increased over the last forty or a hundred years, but his (deflated) income or value added has risen by a factor of four. The barber's increased real income has been generated by activities other than his own. These other activities are much harder on the environment than his own activities. Average Northerners now consume vastly more than they did forty years ago all the way up the income scale: more than twice as much in the case of the United

States and Japan. For example, 88 percent of U.S. households now own one car (up from 55 percent in 1935), and the average number of vehicles per household is two—even for barbers.

7. Subsidized Resource Pricing

The poor can be more directly supported, and with less environmental damage, by "getting the price right," or at least getting the price better than at present. Today's severe underevaluation of Southern raw material exports means the South is subsidizing the North, in the sense of externalized environmental costs, as well as governmental incentives, such as logging-road construction. Cheap tropical log exports are a case in point. Stupendous subsidies, in the form of unpaid environmental costs, are only beginning to be recognized. Eastern Europe's pollution is a case in point. In the absence of Southern cartels or of producers' agreements to limit production, unilateral price changes are unlikely. We therefore advocate that international organizations, such as the World Bank, the International Monetary Fund, and the United Nations, should promote full-cost pricing and foster more economically realistic pricing. Caveat: the North advocates removal of subsidies, but this may hurt the poor more than the rich because, in developing countries, the rate of removal of subsidies to the poor exceeds the rate of removal of subsidies to the rich.

Full-cost pricing should also be used to encourage Southern countries to exploit their comparative advantage in agriculture, labor-intensive industry, and raw-material processing for increasing employment, modernizing their subsistence sectors, and raising their per capita incomes.

8. Inequitable Trading Systems

"The structure of trade . . . is a curse from the perspective of sustainable development," Haavelmo and Hansen (1991) conclude. They elaborate further: "Much Northern growth is based on depleting Southern resources for a price far below the cost of sustainable exploitation. The adoption by the North of the 'full cost' principle for pricing Southern resources would help the South more than would Northern growth. Exports only serve a purpose if they finance useful imports. The North should not [tell] the South to export what it cannot afford. Strategies to enhance exports of many staple agricultural products should be critically revisited. Such goods face low demand elasticities in world markets. Individually each exporter takes the world market price as given. In the aggregate, however, the simultaneous implementation of such strategies by many drives the price down dramatically as they all reach their production targets. In the end the export revenue might fall short of paying for the imported machinery, implements, pesticides, etc., required [to produce] for export."

9. Dysfunctions of Imbalanced Trade

The traditional view tends to overestimate the virtues of free trade— that is, deregulated commerce across national boundaries. Financial imbalances from deregulated trade have led to debts that are unrepayable, and attempts to repay them by rapid export of raw materials can be environmentally destructive. Natural resource stocks are liquidated to meet debt servicing flows. Current efforts under the General Agreement on Tariffs and Trade (GATT) to include services under free trade will subject that sector to international competition, further pressuring existing payment imbalances. There is a conflict between the "free trade" prescription and the "get the price right" prescription. Countries following World Bank advice to internalize external environmental costs should not be expected to engage in free trade with countries that do not follow similar rules of internalization. Tariffs to protect an efficient national policy of cost internalization (not an inefficient industry) should not be ruled out as unwarranted "protectionism." Unpaid environmental costs, such as liquidation of natural capital, are subsidies reducing the price of imports—tantamount to dumping. User costs, from this point of view, should internalize depletion of natural capital. Rectification of the asymmetry of antidumping laws for manufacturers, but not for raw materials, would promote global sustainability. This refers to U.S. Pacific Northwest logs exported to Japan, as well as Malaysian rainforest hardwoods exported to Europe. At the same time, we acknowledge that Southern trade policies have limited intra-South trade in goods and services, which needs to be expanded, and have contributed to real transfers from the rural to urban sectors.

10. The Insecurity of Inequality

From the ecological economic point of view, our main concerns are that the prescription of raising Northern income will fail to alleviate poverty, will worsen inequality, and will reverse current trends toward sustainability. To these ecological economic aspects we append a final concern, that of global security. We believe that raising Northern incomes will decrease global security and, in Minister Emil Salim's Indonesian view, tend to foment social stress and even revolution. Specifically, decreasing sustainability will increase "environmental refugees"—those people forced out of their homes and countries by environmental mismanagement, manmade disasters, and development-induced expulsions, such as poisoned water, air, and soils, as well as erosion and desertification. A specific example is the environmental damage from Papua New Guinea's Panguna copper mine, which was a major cause of the 1989–91 civil war.

The North bears an overwhelming responsibility for many environmental costs to both sinks and sources. As stated in the 1991 Beijing Declaration, the South has taken note that the North is responsible for practically all historical global pollution and continues to emit most of today's global pollution. Some Southern writers—for example, Agarwal and Narain (1991)—argue that the North owes reparation payments to the South for historically disproportionate preemption of the global commons. Reparations are to restore base-line equilibria. Northern security will be enhanced to the extent that the North reduces inequality in the South. North-South environmental linkages are growing. Two examples are instructive. Eastern Europe pollutes Scandinavian air. Scandinavia finds it more cost-effective to improve their own air quality by financing pollution abatement in Eastern Europe rather than in Scandinavia. Similarly, the Netherlands finds it more efficient to sequester Amsterdam-produced carbon dioxide from their coal-fired thermal electricity plants by financing tree plantations in South America. South America gets much employment created and more wood construction materials; the Netherlands buys time to internalize its own wastes within its own borders.

The North should see it as in its own direct security self-interest to invest in the South to reduce inequality, to alleviate Southern poverty, to protect and improve the global environment, and to avoid creating environmental refugees. The South can raise funds by taking on board some of the North's environmental concerns (such as carbon sequestering, in which the tropics have a major additional advantage) by means of tradeable quotas and by selling the benefits gained from use of their environmental assets, such as intact tropical forest. The traditional view advocates appropriating more Southern resources for the North. The alternative view is that the North has to learn to live within its own means, to reduce its current reliance on global commons and on the environmental resources of the South.

Recommendations

Perhaps the major way in which the North can help the South is by adopting the first oath of Hippocrates: "First cease doing harm." The traditional view exacerbates harm; the alternative view is more likely to help. In the global approach to sustainability, the North has to adapt far more than the South. The South's contribution to global sustainability can be focused on population stability and prevention of irreversible losses. The North's contribution to environmental damage in the South is clear—for example, ozone shield damage, climate change, greenhouse warming, tropical deforestation, export plantations that force the poor onto marginal lands, indebtedness that promotes drawdown of natural capital, and overuse of potentially renewable resources.

The primary recommendations for how the North can help the South are:

1. The North should get its own house in order by transforming its present-day consumerism and borrowing economy into a more sustainable model. An accelerated transition to renewable energy for a stable population is the major element. This transition has to be faster than

what would be suggested by the market. A global carbon or nonrenewable energy tax, as proposed by the United Nations Conference on Environment and Development in 1991, and/or tradeable pollution permits (perhaps with futures and options), as proposed by the United Nations Commission on Trade and Development in 1992, would help protect global life-support systems.

2. Northern countries should internalize the costs of disposal of their toxic and other wastes within their own national borders, rather than exporting it in the name of "comparative advantage" to low-wage countries. Internalization of costs to the nation of origin, as well as the firm, gives a stronger incentive to minimize toxic waste generation. This dynamic benefit is more important than the static allocation cost of neglecting "comparative advantage."

3. The North should halt harm to the South perpetuated by present policies. This includes underpricing of Southern exports, warfare, and global pollution.

4. Northern governments, the private sector, and development agencies create significant Southern debt, much of which is unrepayable. The North should address the current imbalance between commercial rate loans, subsidized investments, and grants to the South. The relative proportions of Northern transfers as loans, or as subsidized, almost concessionary, International Development Agency–type arrangements, or essentially as grants, such as by free access by the South to the North's socially and ecologically beneficial technologies, should be improved. Reparations are mentioned above. Questionable loans, those accelerating liquidation of natural capital, those failing to internalize full costs, unrepayable loans, and loans clearly for unsustainable purposes should be canceled or no longer made. Global sustainability, equity, and security would be improved, and poverty eased, if debt were conditionally written off commensurate with environmental progress.

5. As economic justification for foreign exchange loans for environmental investments is difficult or impossible, where international assistance is required for the South's global or transnational environmental priorities, it should be grant funded. Recent World Bank improvements in this respect are encouraging and need to be acceler-

ated. Economists should begin to consider environmental investments as extended infrastructure investments—in other words, investments in the maintenance of the biophysical infrastructure that supports all economic activity, both public and private. Therefore, where conventional cost-benefit analysis is difficult to apply, as in some conventional infrastructure investments, the World Bank, UNDP, and the United Nations Environment Program (UNEP) can now make environmental grants through the pilot Global Environment Facility. This important facility urgently needs to be revised and vastly expanded if it is to help the South to approach sustainability.

6. The North should focus on direct help to the South and away from indirect "trickle down" help. Investments should focus on only the most essential projects, emphasizing domestic needs more than the export market. This means that Official Development Assistance's commercial-rate lending volume to the South would decline. Suggestions to finance such investments have included reparations, conditioned debt relief (for example, the Brady Plan and Trinidad Terms), subsidized loans, and especially grants. The investments are to accelerate needed growth and employment creation in small Southern economies. International assistance is needed to purchase rights to environmentally beneficial technology for the South. As old Northern assets depreciate, some may better be replaced in the South—with appropriate technology. Thus, the North should accelerate export of advanced but appropriate technology for Southern processing of their raw materials.

7. The priorities for sustainable economic development in the South are: acceleration of the transition to population stability; acceleration of the transition to renewable energy; human capital formation (education, training, and employment creation, particularly for girls); technological transfer (to leapfrog the North's environmentally damaging stage of economic evolution) and job creation rather than automation; and direct poverty alleviation, including social safety nets and targeted aid.

Former World Bank President Robert S. McNamara concluded his 1991 United Nations address by calling for official discussion of "how the developed world, consuming seven times as much per capita as do the citizens of the developing countries, may both adjust . . . consumption patterns and reduce the environmental impact of each unit of consumption, so as to help assure a sustainable path of development for all the inhabitants of our planet. It will be neither morally defensible nor politically acceptable to do less."

Acknowledgments

We acknowledge with pleasure the help of our World Bank colleagues, especially Salah El Serafy, as well as that of Roefie Hueting, David Korten, and Raymond Mikesell.

Notes

1. One need is to calculate what fraction of the U.S. $55 billion total annual Official Development Assistance (ODA) supports sustainable investments and increase this expectedly small fraction (disaggregating the large armaments fraction). This should also be done for the possibly U.S. $100 billion that comes annually from philanthropic grants. El Serafy's sustainability method (1991) and environmental accounting (Ahmad, El Serafy, and Lutz 1989) should be widely used.

2. The 1990 "World Development Report: Poverty" calculated that more than 1 billion people—about one-third of the total population in the developing countries—live below the poverty line, and that poverty is also increasing in relative terms (World Bank 1990).

3. The 1989 South to North flows approximated U.S. $50 billion, or U.S. $150 billion by lost trade, excluding "brain drain" costs.

4. The reasons why forty years of capital transfers to the South have not been as successful as planned are: (a) improper allocation of capital, including government expenditures; (b) flawed governmental policies that promoted misallocation, inefficient industries, and urban affluent elites at the expense of the rural sector; (c) large and corrupt bureaucracy and military; (d) neglect of peasant agriculture; and (e) social systems that doom three-fourths of the population, especially women, to an unproductive and stagnating existence, especially

failure to disseminate effective family planning. We are grateful to Raymond Mikesell for this clarification.

5. Resources include the environment as a source of raw materials, healthy air, etc., and as a sink for wastes, such as carbon dioxide.

6. For a discussion of environmental finitude and of sustainability in general, see Daly and Cobb (1989), Daly (1991), Goodland, Daly, and El Serafy (1991), and Goodland and Daly (1992). The two views are best contrasted by Korten (1991) and pithiest by Brooks (1991). For the most recent support for the alternative view, see Krabbe and Heijman (1992).

7. For example, World Bank Vice-President and Chief Economist Lawrence Summers (1991) has commented: "Rising tides do raise all boats." Rising Northern tides presumably imply ebbing Southern tides.

8. Environmental limits to growth can be separated into source limits, such as depletion of petroleum, copper, etc., and sink limits, such as the greenhouse effect, ozone shield damage, pollution, etc.

9. We could add a more palatable modification of the second view, an attack on today's main environmental threat—namely, pollution—by means of effluent charges, standards, etc. This would then be digested efficiently by the market, and one indirect result would likely be a reduction in GDP and throughput. However, this falls into the obscurity of Brundtlandism: that the world needs a "five-to tenfold increase in growth, but of a different kind." While we would support such a frontal attack, we prefer to be crystal clear and opt for a transition away from throughput growth and toward a stable or declining throughput per unit of final product, and for a stable or declining population.

10. For evidence and arguments supporting this important conclusion, see Hueting, Bosch, and de Boer (1992) Appendix 3.

11. This generalization stems from the orders-of-magnitude richer biodiversity in tropical countries and by the related lack of tropical winters. The four main tropical environmental impacts—deracination of jungle dwellers, deforestation, extinctions, and topsoil loss—are irreversible. Water and air pollution in the North are basically reversible. Pervasive global negative externalities (for example, carbon dioxide accumulation) are probably irreversible over most time frames. The operational distinction between reversible and irreversible damage is that cure for the former is possible for the rich; prevention is the only choice for irreversibles.

12. "Impact" here means impact on or damage to environmental sources or sinks; "affluence" means per capita consumption of resources; "technology"

refers to technological efficiency defined in terms of the number of units of human well-being produced per unit of environmental cost. Thus, where I is impact, P is population, and Y is total production, then $I = P \times Y/P \times I/Y$.

13. Data from the World Bank's "World Development Report 1991," Table A.2.

References

Agarwal, A., and S. Narain. "Global Warming in an Unequal World." *International Journal of Sustainable Development* 1(1)(1991): 98–104.

Ahmad, Y., S. El Serafy, and E. Lutz, eds. *Environmental Accounting for Sustainable Development.* Washington, D.C.: World Bank, 1989.

"Beijing Declaration" (Beijing Ministerial Declaration on Environment and Development). Beijing Ministerial Conference of [forty-one ministers of] Developing Countries on Environment and Development, 18–19 June 1991.

Brooks, D. "An Evaluation of 'Our Common Future.'" *Human Economy Newsletter* 12(4)(1991): 4.

Daly, H. E. *Ecological Economics and Sustainable Development: From Concept to Policy.* Environment Department Paper 1991-24. Washington, D.C.: World Bank, 1991.

Daly, H. E., and J. B. Cobb. *For the Common Good: Redirecting the Economy Toward Community, the Environment, and a Sustainable Future.* Boston: Beacon Press, 1989.

Duchin, F. "Prospects for Environmentally Sound Economic Development in the North, in the South, and in North-South Economic Relations: The Role for Action-oriented Analysis." *Journal of Clean Technology and Environmental Sciences.* 1992.

El Serafy, S. "The Environment as Capital." In *Ecological Economics,* edited by R. Costanza. New York: Cambridge University Press, 1991.

Goodland, R., and H. E. Daly. "Approaching Global Environmental Sustainability." *Journal of Society of International Development.* In press.

Goodland, R., H. E. Daly, and S. El Serafy. *Environmentally Sustainable Economic Development: Building on Brundtland.* Environment Department Paper 36. Washington, D.C.: World Bank, 1991.

Haavelmo, T. and S. Hansen. "On the Strategy of Trying to Reduce Economic Inequality by Expanding the Scale of Human Activity." In *Environmen-*

tally *Sustainable Economic Development: Building on Brundtland* (Environment Department Paper 36), edited by Goodland, Daly, and El Serafy. Washington, D.C.: World Bank, 1991.

Hirsch, F. *The Social Limits to Growth.* Cambridge: Harvard University Press, 1976.

Hueting, R. "The Brundtland Report: A Matter of Conflicting Goals." *Ecological Economics* 2 (1990): 109–17.

Hueting, R., P. Bosch, and B. de Boer. *Methodology for the Calculation of Sustainable National Income.* Statistical Essays (M Series). Den Haag: Central Bureau of Statistics, 1992.

Korten, D. C. "Sustainable Development." *World Policy Journal* (Winter 1991–1992): 156–90.

Krabbe, J. J., and W. J. M. Heijman, eds. *National Income and Nature: Externalities, Growth and Steady State.* Dordrecht: Kluwer Academic, 1992.

Meadows, D. H., et al. *The Limits to Growth.* New York: Universe Books, 1974.

McNamara, R. S. "Global Population Policy to Advance Human Development in the 21st Century." New York: United Nations, 1991.

Summers, L. "Research Challenges for Development Economists." *Finance and Development* 28 (September 1991): 2–5.

Tinbergen, J., and R. Hueting. "GNP and Market Prices: Wrong Signals for Sustainable Economic Success That Mask Environmental Destruction." In *Environmentally Sustainable Economic Development: Building on Brundtland* (Environment Department Paper 36), edited by Goodland, Daly, and El Serafy. Washington, D.C.: World Bank, 1991.

United Nations Development Program. "Human Development Report." New York: UNDP, 1992.

World Bank. "World Development Report: Poverty." Washington, D.C.: World Bank, 1990.

Index

About the Authors

Lester R. Brown is president of the Worldwatch Institute.

Robert Costanza is president and founder of the International Society for Ecological Economics and editor-in-chief of *Ecological Economics*.

Herman E. Daly is senior economist in the Environment Department of the World Bank and the author of many works on ecological economics.

Peter Dogsé is associate expert of UNESCO's Division of Ecological Sciences.

Bernd von Droste is director of UNESCO's Division of Ecological Sciences and secretary of the United Nations Man and Biosphere Program.

Salah El Serafy is an economic advisor on the Economic Advisory Staff of the World Bank and has led the Bank into environmental accounting.

Christopher Flavin is a vice-president for research at the Worldwatch Institute.

Robert Goodland is an advisor in the Environment Department of the World Bank and has published more than a dozen books, primarily on tropical ecology.

Trygve Haavelmo is the recipient of the 1989 Nobel Memorial Prize in economics, partly for founding econometrics, and is at the Institute of Economics at the University of Oslo, Norway.

Stein Hansen is director of the Nordic Consulting Group in Oslo, Norway, and a consultant to the World Bank, Asian Development Bank, UNESCO, NORAD, and others.

Roefie Hueting is head of Environmental Statistics at the Netherlands Bureau of Statistics and has been publishing on ecological economics since the 1960s.

Raymond Mikesell is professor of economics at the University of Oregon, Eugene, and has published extensively on trade and development economics and on the economics of natural resources.

Sandra Postel is a vice-president for research at the Worldwatch Institute.

Jan Tinbergen was awarded the first Nobel Memorial Prize in economics in 1969 and was elected first chairman of the United Nations Committee on Development Planning.

Also Available from Island Press

Balancing on the Brink of Extinction: The Endangered Species Act and
Lessons for the Future
Edited by Kathryn A. Kohm

Better Trout Habitat: A Guide to Stream Restoration and Management
By Christopher J. Hunter

Beyond 40 Percent: Record-Setting Recycling and Composting Programs
By The Institute for Local Self-Reliance

Coastal Alert: Ecosystems, Energy, and Offshore Oil Drilling
By Dwight Holing

The Complete Guide to Environmental Careers
By The CEIP Fund

Death in the Marsh
By Tom Harris

Farming in Nature's Image
By Judith Soule and Jon Piper

The Global Citizen
By Donella Meadows

Healthy Homes, Healthy Kids
By Joyce Schoemaker and Charity Vitale

Holistic Resource Management
By Allan Savory

Inside the Environmental Movement: Meeting the Leadership Challenge
By Donald Snow

Learning to Listen to the Land
Edited by Bill Willers

Media and the Environment
Edited by Craig LaMay and Everette E. Dennis

Nature Tourism: Managing for the Environment
Edited by Tensie Whelan

Overtapped Oasis: Reform or Revolution for Western Water
By Marc Reisner and Sarah Bates

Plastics: America's Packaging Dilemma
By Nancy Wolf and Ellen Feldman

The Poisoned Well: New Strategies for Groundwater Protection
Edited by Eric Jorgensen

Race to Save the Tropics: Ecology and Economics for a Sustainable Future
Edited by Robert Goodland

Recycling and Incineration: Evaluating the Choices
By Richard A. Denison and John Ruston

The Rising Tide: Global Warming and World Sea Levels
By Lynne T. Edgerton

The Snake River: Window to the West
By Tim Palmer

Steady-State Economics: Second Edition with New Essays
By Herman E. Daly

Turning the Tide: Saving the Chesapeake Bay
By Tom Horton and William M. Eichbaum

War on Waste: Can America Win Its Battle With Garbage?
By Louis Blumberg and Robert Gottlieb

Wetland Creation and Restoration: The Status of the Science
Edited by Mary E. Kentula and Jon A. Kusler

For a complete catalog of Island Press publications, please write: Island Press, Box 7, Covelo, CA 95428, or call: 1–800–828–1302.

Island Press Board of Directors

SUSAN E. SECHLER, CHAIR
Director
Rural Economic Policy Program
Aspen Institute for Humanistic Studies

HENRY REATH, VICE-CHAIR
President
Collector's Reprints, Inc.

DRUMMOND PIKE, SECRETARY
President
The Tides Foundation

PAIGE K. MACDONALD, ASSISTANT SECRETARY
Executive Vice President/Chief Operating Officer
World Wildlife Fund & The Conservation Foundation

GEORGE T. FRAMPTON, JR., TREASURER
President
The Wilderness Society

ROBERT E. BAENSCH
Senior Vice President/Marketing
Rizzoli International Publications, Inc.

PETER R. BORRELLI
Vice President of Land Preservation
Open Space Institute

CATHERINE M. CONOVER

PAUL HAWKEN
Chief Executive Officer
Smith & Hawken

CHARLES C. SAVITT
President
Center for Resource Economics/Island Press

PETER R. STEIN
Managing Partner
Lyme Timber Company

RICHARD TRUDELL
Executive Director
American Indian Resources Institute